Ripley's Believe It or Not!

2023

Vice President, Licensing & Publishing Amanda Joiner

Creative Content Manager Sabrina Sieck

Editor Jordie R. Orlando

Text Geoff Tibballs

Feature Contributors Engrid Barnett, Jordie R. Orlando

Proofreaders Rachel Paul, Yvette Chin

Fact-checker & Indexer Yvette Chin

Special Thanks Tacita Barrera, Yaneisy Contreras, John Corcoran, Steph Distasio, Barbara Faurot, Colton Kruse, Matt Mamula, Julia Moellmann, and Kurtis Moellmann

Designer Luis Fuentes

Reprographics Bob Prohaska

Cover Artwork Rose Audette

ISBN 978-1-529-13631-9

First published in Great Britain in 2022 by Century

Century
20 Vauxhall Bridge Road
London SW1V 2SA

www.penguin.co.uk

Century is part of the Penguin Random House group of companies whose addresses can be found at global.penguinrandomhouse.com

ISBN 978-1-529-13631-9
10 9 8 7 6 5 4 3 2 1

Vice President, Licensing & Publishing
Ripley Entertainment Inc.
7576 Kingspointe Parkway, Suite 188
Orlando, Florida 32819
publishing@ripleys.com

A CIP catalogue record for this book is available from the British Library.

Printed in China by Leo Paper

PUBLISHER'S NOTE
While every effort has been made to verify the accuracy of the entries in this book, the Publishers cannot be held responsible for any errors contained in the work. They would be glad to receive any information from readers.

WARNING
Some of the stunts and activities in this book are undertaken by experts and should not be attempted by anyone without adequate training and supervision.

Ripley's Believe It or Not!

ESCAPE THE ORDINARY

2023

RIPLEY PUBLISHING

a Jim Pattison Company

ESCAPE THE

To become the man behind the "Ripley's Believe It or Not!" name, Robert Ripley first had to *Escape the Ordinary!*

Born in 1890, Robert Ripley grew up in the hills of Santa Rosa, California, as an energetic but shy kid. Mocked for his large front teeth and stutter, he found an escape in the form of drawing. His artistic abilities took him to New York City, where he became a sports cartoonist for *The New York Globe* newspaper. (Back in those days, cameras weren't fast enough to capture speedy movements, so instead, illustrators like Ripley would recreate important moments in sports with an artistic flair.)

On a slow news day in 1918, Ripley gathered nine out-of-the-ordinary athletic feats and put them all together in a cartoon panel he called "Champs and Chumps." He was taking a chance, but his readers loved it! Ripley soon returned to the concept and retitled the series *Believe It or Not*.

Within just a few years, newspapers began sponsoring Ripley to travel the globe, not to illustrate sports news, but to gather strange tales from far-off places. Unlike today—where you can talk to someone on the other side of the planet with just a tap on a screen—people in the 1920s did not have easy access to foreign places. Instead, Ripley brought the world to his readers through their newspaper, and eventually their radios, TVs, bookstores, and more.

Today, Robert Ripley's legacy lives on—from the *Believe It or Not!* cartoon still published daily more than 100 years later and the museums around the world that bear his name, to the book you're holding in your hands and more. Before he could achieve the extraordinary, he first had to do something unusual—he had to *Escape the Ordinary!*

NEHI NEWS

WARM DAYS AHEAD
MORE BUSINESS
GREATER PROFITS

STUDY YOUR SALES
MANUAL. IT MEANS
MONEY TO YOU.

Volume 7, No. 3 — MARCH, 1940 — Columbus, Ga.

RADIO PROGRAM HITS NEW POPULARITY PEAK

After a series of spectacular broadcasts, which moved at a fast clip, ROYAL CROWN'S CBS 88-station coast-to-coast radio program featuring "Believe-It-Or-Not" Bob Ripley has hit a new popularity peak. Following the opener in New York February 16th, Ripley and the cast sojourned to Florida, where two outstanding programs were broadcast. The listening audience has steadily increased and the program is now rated one of the top half-hour shows on the air.

Stimulated by scores of favorable program reviews, which include the prized Variety and Radio Daily columns, and innumerable letters and gratifying expressions from ROYAL CROWN Bottlers, the cast is determined to march the program to an even greater height.

The St. Augustine, Florida, "Marine Studio" program was heralded a broadcast triumph by many radio columnists, and proved an exciting venture for Bob Ripley and the listeners. The daring presentation won a number of hearty program endorsements and many letters stated that ROYAL CROWN was putting thrill into radio listening.

In pictorial form we review the highlights of the program broadcast from Marineland—located near St. Augustine, Florida.

TOO LATE NOW! Bob Ripley dons the diver's suit... willingly but not enthusiastically.

TO SHARK-INFESTED WATERS! Down in the deep he goes to tell the world how it feels to meet a man-eating shark face to face.

A HUNGRY PORPOISE FED BY HAND! Lurching forward at great speed, the mammal feeds from human hands.

WE'RE ON THE AIR! Action and thrills are sent through these radio engineers to over a million listening radio fans.

ORDINARY

J. DARBY of England—JUMPED BACKWARDS 12 ft. 11 in. (with weights)

R.P. WILLIAMS MADE A RUNNING HIGH KICK of 10 ft. 3 in. (New London, Conn.-1905)

MIRROR

H.HILLMAN and LAWSON ROBERTSON DID 100 yds. IN 11 Secs. IN A THREE-LEGGED RACE

REMEMBER THE CHAP WHO WALKED BACKWARDS ACROSS THE CONTINENT?

BLUB

M. PAULIQUEN, Paris-1912 REMAINED UNDER WATER 6 Min. 29 4/5 Secs.

J.M. BARNETT of Australia—JUMPED THE ROPE 11,810 TIMES.—(About 4 hours)

ED. LAMY BROAD-JUMPED ON ICE— 25 ft. 7 in. (Saranac Lake) 1913.

A. FORRESTER of Toronto—RAN 100 Yds. BACKWARDS IN 14 seconds

S.D. SEE HOPPED 100 YDS. IN 11 seconds.

THE FIRST *BELIEVE IT OR NOT!* CARTOON!

Built around the adventures of Robert Ripley and his travels across the globe searching for extraordinary people, unusual artifacts, and unbelievable stories, Ripley's Attractions always have something new for curious minds to discover!

With more than 100 attractions across four continents—from **Odditoriums** and **Waxworks** to **Moving Theaters** and **Aquariums**—the world of Ripley's continues to grow through exciting new experiences! In 2021, go-kart–centric Ripley's Super Fun Park in Pigeon Forge, Tennessee, got off to the races, while Cancún got its very own Ripley's Believe It or Not! Odditorium!

CAN YOU CANCÚN?

The newest Odditorium to join the Ripley's Believe It or Not! family can be found in **Cancún, Mexico**! Located in La Isla Shopping Village, guests can explore 11 immersive galleries packed with more than 400 artifacts from around the world. The Odditorium completes the Ripley's Attraction trifecta at La Isla, where visitors can also experience Ripley's Marvelous Mirror Maze and Ripley's LaseRace!

EMBRACE THE WEIRD

Florida has a reputation for being, well, a little unusual sometimes. So, our Orlando Odditorium decided to celebrate its strange side with their new **Weird Florida** gallery! Featured within are exhibits you won't find anywhere else, like a shrunken torso owned by famous novelist—and former Key West resident—Ernest Hemingway, as well as an ancient fossilized alligator!

The Ripley's Believe It or Not! Odditorium in **Branson, Missouri**, got a brand-new look worthy of your favorite makeover show!

ADRENALINE RUSH

The latest Ripley's Attraction in Tennessee is sure to rev your engine! **Ripley's Super Fun Park** features multiple go-kart tracks, with the largest climbing multiple levels above the ground. When you're not burning rubber, battle your friends aboard Blaster Boats equipped with water cannons or challenge them to a game inside the 10,000-square-foot (929-sq-m) arcade!

MORE THAN MEETS THE EYE

The mind-bending cover of this book was inspired in part by our belief that "normal" is just an illusion. No two people are exactly alike, so what may appear normal from one person's point of view might be totally bizarre for someone else! In honor of this philosophy, Ripley's opened a brand-new attraction in 2022. At **Ripley's Illusion Lab** in San Antonio, Texas, visitors are invited to step into a world of optical trickery and see things from a totally new perspective!

THINKING OUT OF THE BOX

kids invent stuff

For the launch of last year's book, *Ripley's Believe It or Not! Out of the Box,* we teamed up with Kids Invent Stuff and challenged creative kids to submit their unusual invention ideas for the chance to have their contraption brought to life!

The winning design was a floor-mopping dinosaur imagined by nine- and ten-year-old sister duo Kelsey and Lexi from the UK. The engineers behind Kids Invent Stuff, Ruth and Shawn, quickly got to work building this out-of-the-box creation. The final result? A 7-foot-tall (2.1-m) robotic *T. rex* made of foam and resin capable of cleaning up the nastiest of spills!

HOW IT'S GOING!

HOW IT STARTED.

ROBOT T-REX CLEANER

ORANGE YOU GLAD?

If you've never seen a live lobster, you might not know that they are usually dark brown in color before transforming into that iconic shade of red when cooked. But in September 2021, Niki Lundquist of Whitby, Ontario, spotted a bright orange lobster swimming in the seafood tank at a grocery store—a one-in-30-million rarity! To save him from being eaten, Niki purchased the crustacean—which she dubbed "Pinchy"—and brought him to Ripley's Aquarium of Canada, where he has been living happily ever since!

CREATING THE WORLD'S LARGEST
BALL OF HUMAN HAIR

Ripley's fans first met Hoss the Human Hairball in the pages of *Ripley's Believe It or Not! A Century of Strange!*, when he weighed a scant 96 pounds (43.5 kg).

Well, Hoss went on a weight-gain journey and is now officially the Guinness World Records™ title holder for Largest Ball of Human Hair!

THE BEGINNING

Hoss was initially created by Steve Warden, a hair stylist from Ohio who was inspired by other odd Believe It or Not! feats. After being featured himself, Steve gifted Hoss to Ripley's in 2018.

FOR A GOOD CAUSE

With a pandemic beard in full-effect, President of Ripley's Believe It or Not!, Jim Pattison Jr., decided to contribute his own hair to Hoss, launching Ripley's Shave the Beard and Make it Weird challenge to raise money for Give Kids The World Village.

MAIL IN YOUR MANE

Thousands of people mailed in their manes to Ripley's HQ and visited Floyd's 99 Barbershops of Florida to help reach the record.

RECORD-BREAKER

By December 2021, Hoss achieved the Guinness World Records™ title of Largest Ball of Human Hair at a whopping 225.13 pounds (102.12 kg)!

HOSS THE HUMAN HAIRBALL

HAPPY NEW YEAR!

To ring in 2022, Ripley's even streamed a New Year's Eve ball drop featuring Hoss!

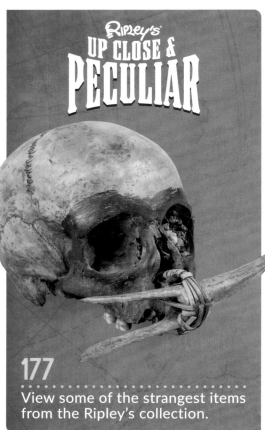

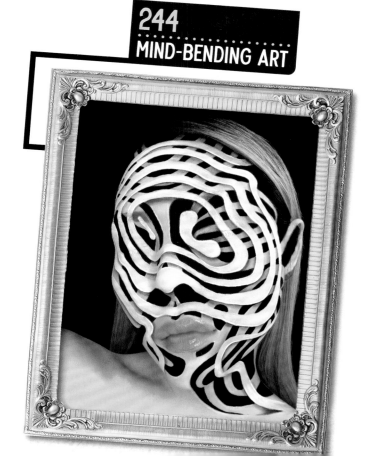

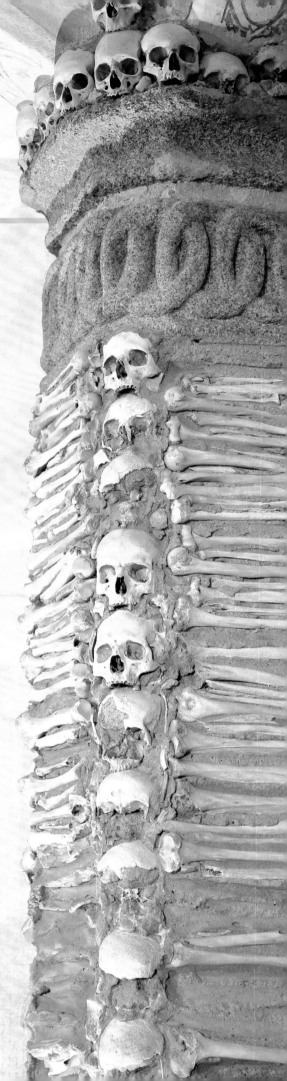

TRANSPARENT TRANSPORT

Created in 1939, the Pontiac Ghost Car was the first full-sized transparent automobile ever manufactured in the United States.

Engineers designed the vehicle to accompany the "Highways and Horizons" pavilion built by General Motors for the New York World's Fair. Its see-through plastic construction meant visitors to the exhibit could see everything from the structural metal to the spare tire. The only thing missing from the clear car was insulation, which is normally included to help lower heat and sound.

HOME TREADMILL
While working from home, Yves Hanoulle, from Ghent, Belgium, walked 932 miles (1,500 km) in three months by using a treadmill placed under his standing desk. He averaged around 27,000 steps every day.

JENGA TOWER
Building upward from the base of a single vertical Jenga block, Tai Star Valianti, of Pima, Arizona, stacked 485 blocks to form a tower in the shape of an inverted pyramid. It took him around two hours to build and stood on its own for nine minutes until it was demolished by his young son.

GHOST HUNTER
Nineteenth-century novelist Charles Dickens was a ghostbuster! He was a member of London's Ghost Club, which hunted ghosts and investigated reports of paranormal happenings and hauntings.

COBAIN CARDIGAN
A stained, cigarette-burned cardigan worn by Kurt Cobain for Nirvana's MTV *Unplugged* performance in 1993—and never washed since—sold at auction in New York in 2019 for $334,000.

EYEBALL TATTOOS
Amber Luke, from New South Wales, Australia, has more than 250 tattoos covering her entire body and face—including her eyeballs, which are inked bright blue. She has spent more than $30,000 on designs that feature animals, skulls, flowers, and block patterns. She also has a split tongue and silicone implants in her ears to make her look like a pixie.

EYE WIDE OPEN

Everything's bigger in Texas, and this proves no less true in downtown Dallas, where you'll find a 30-foot-tall (9.1-m) lifelike sculpture of a human eyeball, red veins and all. *The Eye* was created by Tony Tasset in 2007; he fabricated the giant orb from fiberglass. After its initial display, the peeper spent a few years in storage and made a brief appearance in St. Louis, Missouri, before returning to Texas in 2013, where it remains on permanent lookout.

PECULIAR PINEAPPLE

Dave and Angie Kaffenberger of Big Pine Key, Florida, sent us the story of a strange fruit they grew in their yard. At first glance, the odd produce looks like conjoined pineapples gone wild. But a closer inspection reveals a heart-shaped fused fruit. The peculiar growth is called "fasciation" and is unpredictable, resulting from abnormal activity in the growing tip of the plant. In this case, it makes for one delicious-looking tropical treat!

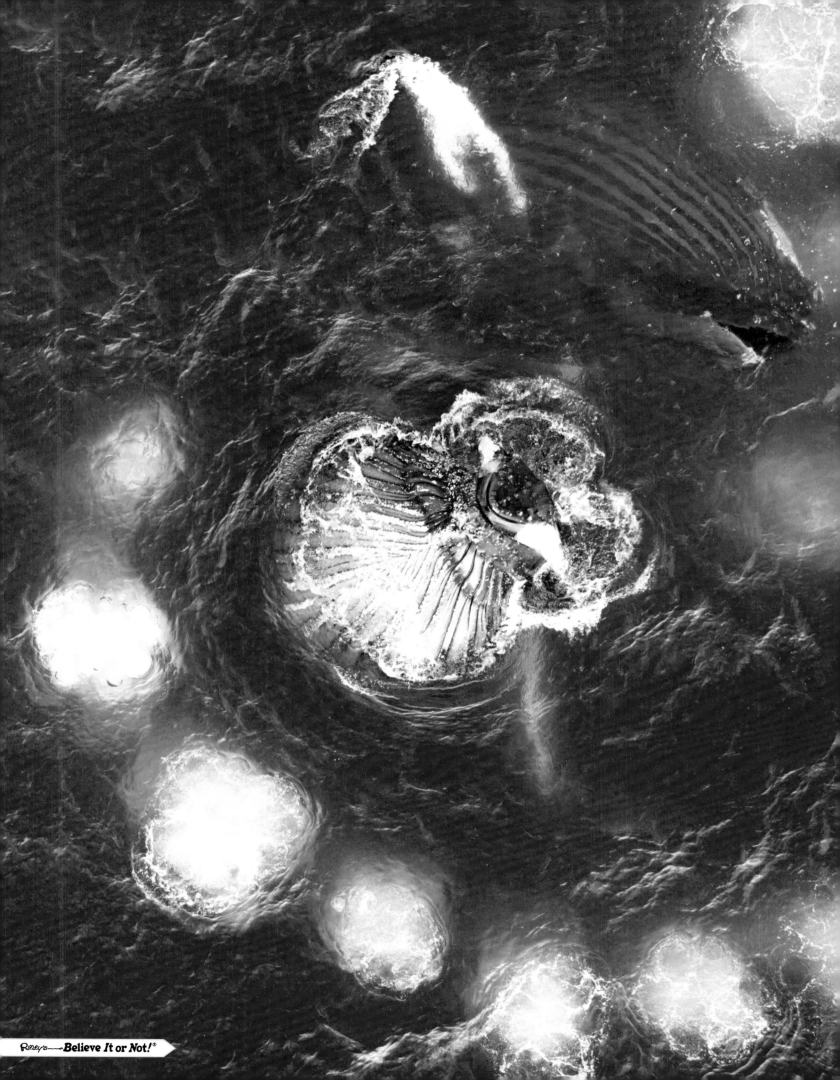

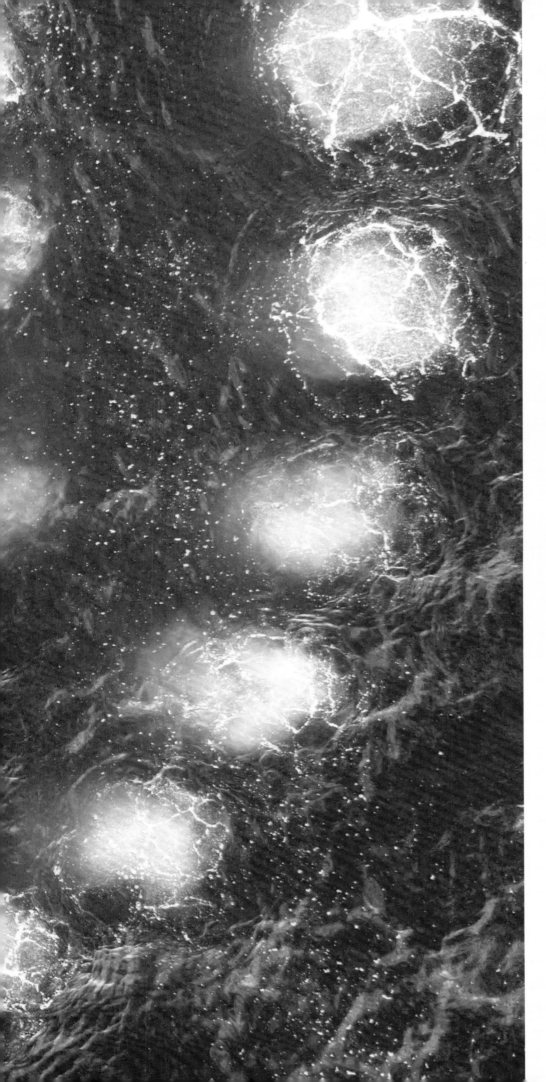

BUBBLE BUFFET

Humpback whales have developed an ingenious technique called "bubble net hunting" to ensure the biggest catch with each bite.

How does "bubble net hunting" work? Swimming upward in a spiral motion, whales blow bubbles beneath the water. In effect, they create a net of bubbles, making it difficult for fish to escape. The whales then reinforce any holes they find in the "net" with their flippers, keeping the fish inside. Then it's just a matter of swimming up from below the net and devouring the yummy, fishy goodness in a massive gulp. Believe it or not, humpback whales can eat up to 3,000 pounds (1,360 kg) in a single day! Talk about making the most of each meal!

NOT-SO-NOBLE NICKNAMES

From Catherine the Great to Richard the Lion-Hearted, some monarchs have all the luck regarding the nicknames they inspire.

But there are some ineffective, unlucky, or ruthless leaders who ended up with less-than-flattering monikers. The most unfortunate of these nobles could never shake the name-calling marring their reputations and legacies. Here are some of the doozies people still talk about today.

THE CABBAGE

Tsar Ivaylo of Bulgaria was born a peasant but rose to the highest ranks by leading an uprising in northeastern Bulgaria. So, you might think his subjects would call him something grandiose or majestic. Instead, they went counterintuitive, referring to him as "The Cabbage," a genuinely humble vegetable.

THE BALD

Few people with a receding hairline voluntarily draw attention to the thinning. But King Charles II of France and the Holy Roman Empire couldn't escape it. His subjects called him "The Bald." The jury is still out on how he got this epithet, but considering baldness inspired open ridicule and laughter in the ninth century, we're guessing it didn't thrill him.

THE TERRIBLE

In 1547, Tsar Ivan IV of Russia received the official title "Tsar and Grand Prince of All of Russia." While there's nothing too shabby about this moniker, the Tsar's subjects had another name for him: "The Terrible." The title didn't come out of nowhere—Ivan IV had violent outbursts of rage, suffered from paranoia, and even murdered his own son.

BLOODY MARY

When Queen Mary I ascended the English throne, her subjects had high hopes for a peaceful and prosperous reign. But her determination to steer the nation back under papal control led to vicious persecution and the martyrdom of countless English Protestants. A violence-stained rule led to a nasty name: "The Bloody."

THE DO-NOTHING

The last leader of the Carolingian dynasty enjoyed an uneventful and disappointing career. Crowned King Louis V in 979 AD, he distinguished himself among his subjects as "The Do-Nothing." Ouch! In all fairness, he died heirless at the age of 20 after a hunting accident, leaving him little time to blossom as a monarch. Nevertheless, his zero-sum reputation never budged.

GVGLIELMO cognominato il Malo, morti gli altri fratelli, succeffe nel Regno a Ruggiero ſuo padre già detto: ei viffe 46 anni, e ne regnò 15. effendo morto nel 1164.

THE MAD

In 1380, King Charles VI of France took the throne at just 11 years old. A mere eight years later, he became the sole sovereign of the nation. In his twenties, he began experiencing unfortunate psychotic episodes that would plague him his entire life, including periods during which he believed he was made of glass. This earned him the title "The Mad."

THE BAD

King William I of Sicily encouraged religious tolerance, promoted science and learning, and created an efficient government. But he also undercut the centralized authority of Sicily's barons and lost the nation's African landholdings to rebellion. The result? He bore the shame of a simple yet cruel nickname: "The Bad."

THE LOUSY

The first king of Norway was anything but proactive when it came to personal hygiene. He refused to cut his hair for a decade before taking the throne, leading to unwanted consequences. These included lice infestations, resulting in the unflattering name "Harald, the Lousy."

FOAM HOME

If you ever spot mini masses of frothy, sticky bubbles on the leaves in your garden come springtime, then you know spittlebug nymphs (a.k.a. froghoppers) have been at work. Some froghoppers may produce as many as 80 bubbles per minute, and the foam protects them from drying out in low humidity environments, temperature extremes, and predators. While in their bubbles, spittlebugs don't have to breathe—an incredible adaptation to their environment!

38 CENTS

How much money Tom's Diner in Denver, Colorado, charges their customers for asking a "stupid question."

PIZZA BOXES

Pizza delivery driver Randy DeGregorio, of Manalapan, New Jersey, can fold 18 cardboard pizza boxes in one minute.

238 FLAVORS

La Casa Gelato, an ice cream shop in Vancouver, British Columbia, Canada, serves 238 different flavors—including roasted garlic and chocolate bacon.

RING MYSTERY

In 1973, Debra McKenna accidentally left her future husband Shawn's class ring in a store restroom in Portland, Maine, but it was found by a metal detectorist 47 years later in a forest in Kaarina, Finland—3,750 miles (6,000 km) away. Although Shawn had visited Finland in the 1990s, it was a long way from where the ring was found and he had not seen the ring for 20 years by that time.

FOG WARNING

Robert Foulis invented the steam-powered foghorn after he was walking toward his house in Saint John, New Brunswick, Canada, on a foggy night in 1853 and heard his daughter playing the piano. Realizing he could only hear the very low notes of the piano, he devised an instrument that emitted a low frequency sound to warn ships approaching harbor in dense fog.

AVOCADO SPILL

A stretch of Interstate 10 in Guadalupe County, Texas, was closed for several hours on October 29, 2019, when a semitruck rolled over and spilled 40,000 pounds (18,144 kg) of avocados onto the highway.

Crater City

The Bavarian town of Nördlingen, Germany, sits atop a massive meteorite crater.

The town's first inhabitants settled at the site in 898 AD, and by the Middle Ages, townspeople constructed a wall around the city to protect it. The meteor's initial impact created suevite, a rough-grained stone containing crystal, glass, and diamonds. The city's church, constructed from suevite, contains about 5,000 carats worth of diamonds, and researchers estimate that the entire townsite is embedded with 72,000 tons of tiny diamonds! However, they're too small to be of great value.

SAFETY PIN PIN STYLE

Fascinated by daily objects and how to best repurpose them to display their beauty, Tonje Halvorsen of Saltsjö-Boo, Sweden, has fashioned safety pin clothing and accessories since 2014.

After ordering 100,000 safety pins, she crafted her first piece of wearable art, an intricate process that quickly devoured her free time. By 2019, she exhibited her first collection, aptly titled *Obsession*. All told, Tonje utilized 500,000 safety pins and 1.5 million beads and sequins to create it. She also dedicated 7,000 hours to completing the collection's 21 garments. The safety pin hobby now a full-blown addiction, Tonje quit her job to devote herself to this prickly passion.

LOOKING SHARP

For the chic French Revolutionary who had everything, the perfect gift in 1793 included guillotine earrings. Commemorating the beheading of King Louis XVI and created at the height of the French Terror, each of the tiered earrings featured a Phrygian cap (a symbol of liberty) at the top, followed by a guillotine and an upside-down decapitated head. Between June 1793 and July 1794, roughly 17,000 executions took place. Clearly, the only thing trendier than death by blade were these sharp-looking accessories.

EXPENSIVE PARASITE
Yartsa gunbu, a parasitic fungus in Tibet that infects ghost moth caterpillars, sells for up to $50,000 a pound on account of its supposed medicinal properties.

DELAYED DELIVERY
Elliot Berinstein was puzzled when Canada Post delivered a package that he wasn't expecting to his Toronto home in May 2020. When he looked inside, he saw it was a hair cream product that he had ordered eight years earlier, along with a 2012 receipt.

GIRAFFE COSTUME
When Mrs. He ran out of protective face masks during the COVID-19 pandemic, she went to the hospital in Luzhou, China, to collect vital medication for her father wearing an inflatable giraffe costume. The costume covered her entire body from head to toe, leaving just a small area of plastic film halfway down the giraffe's neck for her to see out of.

PAPER BIRDS

Niharika Rajput, an artist from New Delhi, India, makes incredibly detailed, life-size sculptures of birds using a wire frame and thousands of tiny pieces of paper. A bird can take several months to complete because she has to cut each body, wing, and tail feather individually from pastel paper and glue them into place one at a time.

MONKEY SELFIES

After Zackrydz Rodzi's phone went missing from his home in Batu Pahat, Malaysia, he found it in a wooded area behind his yard loaded with monkey selfies! The monkey had apparently crept into Rodzi's bedroom while he was asleep, taken the phone outside, and while playing with it had snapped selfie photos and videos.

HEAD WOUND

While diving for prehistoric shark teeth in Florida's Myakka River, Jeffrey Heim was bitten on the head by a 9-foot-long (2.7-m) alligator, leaving him with a minor skull fracture and needing 34 staples in the wound. He would almost certainly have drowned if the gator had grabbed him and gone into a death roll.

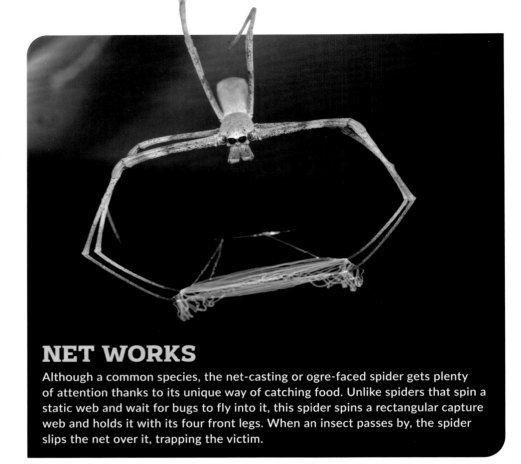

NET WORKS

Although a common species, the net-casting or ogre-faced spider gets plenty of attention thanks to its unique way of catching food. Unlike spiders that spin a static web and wait for bugs to fly into it, this spider spins a rectangular capture web and holds it with its four front legs. When an insect passes by, the spider slips the net over it, trapping the victim.

TINY BOAT

Researchers from Leiden University in the Netherlands used an electron microscope and a 3D printer to create a tiny model boat that was just 30 micrometers in length (0.00118 inches)—so small it could sail down the inside of a human hair.

EXPANDING QUEEN

A termite queen lays an egg every three seconds for up to 20 years, causing her body to distend rapidly from the size of a dime to the size of a human index finger. When her usefulness is over, her offspring lick her to death, drawing the fluids and fats out of her body.

PENCIL LEADS

Chien-Chu Lee, an artist from Taiwan, used a magnifying glass to create a chain of 168 tiny links from the graphite of a single pencil. He has also carved tiny replicas of the Eiffel Tower and the Great Wall of China plus the entire English alphabet into pencil leads.

STRATEGIC PLACEMENT

Like many plants, carnivorous species such as Venus flytraps are pollinated by insects. But how do they make sure they don't accidentally eat these little helpers? By growing their flowers far from their traps! When observing the kinds of insects that visit carnivorous plants, researchers have found that there is very little overlap between the species that pollinate the plants and the insects targeted by the traps.

FUNG-DYE

The green elfcup fungus stands out with its vibrant turquoise hues and ability to stain forest wood a verdant shade.

This stained wood is known as "green oak." During its heyday in the eighteenth and nineteenth centuries, "green oak" was prized by craftsmen for its appearance. Used in fine woodworking, artisans create exquisite patterns by inlaying this wood with other colors and wood grains.

SUSPENDED IN TIME

Laurence, a prop maker and creator of Whathowhy on social media, suspends everyday objects—from hot dogs to Big Macs, lightbulbs to iPhones—in acrylic, crafting fascinating art pieces.

What inspired Laurence to preserve items in acrylic? The opportunity to create a time capsule for future generations, allowing viewers to understand objects in their entirety from every possible angle. Since crafting his first masterpiece by suspending a hot dog in acrylic, he's attracted a massive social media following. In the process, he's also pioneered a fascinating and unique way to catalog the items most of us take for granted.

"Encasing items in acrylic provides a uniquely uniform way to catalog objects and food."

Q. What was the first non-traditional item you encased, and what inspired you to preserve it?
A. The first item I chose to cast in acrylic was a hot dog. Having figured out the best technique for organic matter casting, I had to test it on this frank. Interestingly, it went on to become famous online, specifically Reddit. With many people checking up on the hot dog each month, we built a small community based on the project with thousands of members. From this, everything followed!

Q. *When it comes to preserving something for future generations, how is encasing it in acrylic different from, say, taking a picture or video?*

A. For me, being able to actually hold things in my hands and use a tactile sense to fully take in an object is very important; this is why children always want to touch things at museums. We learn a lot from how we physically interact with the world. Encasing items in acrylic provides a uniquely uniform way to catalog objects and food.

Q. *Is there a way to remove items from the acrylic once it has dried?*

A. No, the acrylic is completely inert and extremely hard once cured. This is part of the reason I use it for preservation, as it is very good at protecting the objects. In fact, some bulletproof glass is created using layers of the same kind of plastic I use.

Q. WHAT ARE THE TOP ITEMS YOU'VE ENCASED IN THE FOLLOWING CATEGORIES?

Most expensive: Apple Watch
Most difficult: Bowl of cereal
Most popular: Hot dog
Personal favorite: Big Mac

PURPLE WONDER

Resembling a night sky speckled with stars, this amethyst geode towers at an alarming 16.4 feet (5 m) tall—as tall as a giraffe! Scattered throughout like tiny yellow planets are rare spherical calcite crystals. The impressive geologic curiosity was found in Uruguay, a common site for geodes, and weighs in at about 14 tons. A geode is a rock that formed around organic material or gas, which decays or dissipates, leaving a hollow center in which minerals like amethyst can grow.

GRENADE FISHING

While attempting to locate a lost rod, magnet fisherman Che Williams pulled 19 World War II hand grenades out of the River Tame near Birmingham, England. Two of the grenades still had their pins in place, causing the surrounding area to be evacuated.

LOST WALLET

In 1968, Paul Grisham of San Diego, California, lost his wallet while working as a meteorologist with the U.S. Navy at McMurdo Station in Antarctica—and 53 years later the wallet was returned to him after being found during the demolition of a building at the station.

COLLEGE PRANK

A bronze sword that was stolen from a Westfield, Massachusetts, statue of Revolutionary War General William Shepard in 1980 as a college prank was returned 40 years later by the remorseful thief.

PINK LADY

Swiss teacher Yasmin Charlotte surrounds herself with the color pink. Her entire apartment is decorated pink, including furniture, curtains, carpets, and chandeliers. If she finds something she likes in a different color, she simply paints it pink. She only ever wears pink clothes and owns more than 100 pairs of pink shoes.

PAINTED NAILS

Thirty-five students in Michoacán, Mexico, allegedly tried to cheat on their entrance exam into schools for teachers by painting onto their fingernails a colored dot pattern that corresponded to the correct answers of the multiple-choice questions.

HIGH LOW

The lowest natural point in Switzerland, Ascona on Lake Maggiore, is still 643 feet (196 m) above sea level—making it higher than Denmark's highest natural point, the 560-foot-tall (171-m) hill named Møllehøj.

LARVAE SNACK

Served as a popular street food in Laos and Cambodia, bee honeycomb is wrapped in banana leaves, grilled, and served with the larvae still inside.

HISTORIC FLOOR

The floor of Amazon founder Jeff Bezos's home in Beverly Hills, California, contains the very floorboards on which French statesman Napoleon Bonaparte was standing when he proposed to Josephine over 200 years ago.

LAST WORDS

As Shay Bradley's coffin was lowered into the ground in Kilmanagh, Ireland, a recording of him shouting, "Hello, hello! Let me out!" was played to mourners. The message was recorded before the jokester's death and broadcast through a speaker at the cemetery.

SPACE CROP PRODUCTION

PH-04

ESPAÑOLA IMPROVED

PH-04: HATCH TO ISS · NASA KSC

SPACE TACOS

For the first time in history, astronauts aboard the International Space Station grew chile peppers and then harvested them to garnish their food on taco night.

Growing these spicy treats proved to be a serious challenge compared to previous crops cultivated in space. To help the plants during their lengthy growing season, researchers back home on planet Earth closely monitored the plants using the Advanced Plant Habitat's 180 controls and sensors. Of course, the space astronauts also lent a hand to the project, resulting in what NASA astronaut Megan McArthur referred to as the "best space tacos yet!"

"BEST SPACE TACOS YET!"

![Ripley's Up Close & Peculiar]

Ripley's Exhibit
Cat. No. 175161

SMIDGET

One of the smallest horses to ever live, Smidget weighed just 75 pounds (34 kg) and stood 21 inches (53 cm) tall. Born on April 13, 1979, in Jackson, Michigan, she gained fame for her starring role as the unicorn in the television series *Faerie Tale Theatre*. She also traveled the U.S., meeting celebrities and performing tricks on national talk shows along the way.

ONLY 21 INCHES (53 CM) TALL!

Ripley's——*Believe It or Not!*®

TWISTED RABBIT

Gary Hubbard of Virginia once owned a pet rabbit that could tilt its head 180 degrees to the side. This feat made the creature's head appear to be upside-down! Believe it or not, Hubbard claimed the rabbit could even eat with its head like this.

EXTRA LONG DEER

This abnormal creature measures about 5.4 feet (1.7 m) long and 4.3 feet (1.3 m) tall. While typical white-tailed deer can grow longer, it is the unusual proportions and narrow width of about 13 inches (33 cm) that make this specimen unique.

CASH FIND

While driving on a road in Goochland County, Virginia, David and Emily Schantz ran over two bags containing nearly $1 million in cash. At first, they thought the bags were filled with trash so they threw them in the back of their pickup truck, but when they arrived back at their home in Caroline County, they discovered the money and handed it over to the local sheriff's office.

GOLD HAUL

While staying in their late grandmother's home in Vendôme, France, in 2020, two young brothers decided to build a hut in the garden, using tree branches and bed sheets—but when they fetched the sheets from a spare room, two gold bars fell out! It turned out that the grandmother had secretly purchased the bars in 1967 and they were now worth more than $100,000.

14 FROGS

The number of Loa water frogs remaining in the world, all found living in a small brown puddle near Calama, Chile.

CHILD GENIUS

Kashe Quest, the daughter of Sukhjit Athwal and Devon Quest from Los Angeles, California, had an IQ of 146 at age two, allowing her to be accepted into Mensa, the world high-IQ society. Her score was about 50 points higher than the U.S. average for all ages. She could identify all 50 states by shape, name the elements on the periodic table, and recognize 50 signs in sign language.

PLANET NAME

The former planet Pluto was named by an 11-year-old girl—Venetia Burney, from Oxford, England. Her librarian grandfather knew a number of astronomers, and in 1930 her idea, inspired by the mythological god of the underworld, was adopted by the Royal Astronomical Society, which had been struggling to find a name for the newly discovered planet.

TULIP SUNDAES

The ice cream tulip will have you licking your lips, thanks to the fact that it looks like a pink bowl filled with fluffy scoops of vanilla ice cream. Why the mouthwatering good looks? The flowers are double-petaled, containing a minimum of a dozen apiece, and the white centers rarely open all the way, maintaining the delicious sundae appearance.

ROCK ON

For the past five decades, Italian artist Luigi Lineri has amassed a vast collection of stones resembling human faces, fish, and animals.

Although he has yet to formally count the entire collection, he's organized each piece based on its shape and appearance. Each shape in his collection numbers in the thousands, and he collects them along the Adige River, located in northern Italy's Verona. Luigi hypothesizes that the stones may have been shaped by prehistoric human beings. When he began this work, Luigi never intended to fill his home with so many rocks. But he has come to consider the collection his "most beautiful piece of poetry."

Fish-shaped stones

EGGS-TRAORDINARY EGGS!

All birds, most insects, many sea creatures, and even a couple mammals lay eggs, rather than give birth to live young.

However, not all eggs look like the kind you buy from a grocery store. Many are highly specialized to give the creatures growing inside them the greatest chance of survival. From strange colors and odd shapes to bizarre defense mechanisms, here are some of the strangest eggs in the animal kingdom.

MOSQUITOS

Imagine shrinking to the size of a mosquito. Specks of soot measuring between 0.13 and 0.25 inches (0.32 and 0.64 cm) wide on the water's surface would suddenly appear as well-organized rafts containing between 100 and 300 eggs. Mosquitos lay these "rafts" anywhere there's water, from tin cans to ornamental ponds and even horse troughs.

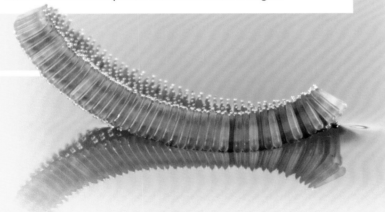

SAND SNAILS

If you find yourself on an Australian beach staring down a long, clear plop of jelly, you've likely crossed paths with "sausage blubber" or "shark poo." While creative, these names don't indicate what's inside. What are these transparent sacs? Sand snail egg cases housing hundreds of babies!

PRAYING MANTISES

Praying mantis mothers lay their eggs in brown, polystyrene-looking structures. Known as *oothecae*, these tan, foamy masses appear in the fall, perfectly insulating the eggs from cold and predators. Once the mantis nymphs hatch, they remain in the case for between three and six months before emerging.

LACEWINGS

Green lacewings have a neat trick to keep their eggs from getting devoured by ants. They lay the little white dots on the tips of tiny silken threads, just long enough to keep ants out of reach. Some lacewings take it a step further, adding chemical defenses to their suspended nests.

DIAMOND SQUIDS

While the egg sacs of diamond squids look like giant underwater slinkies, these structures protect up to 40,000 tiny pink eggs! Found in places like Australia's Great Barrier Reef, they can easily measure more than 6 feet (1.8 m) long, making for a rare and incredible discovery beneath the waves.

SHARKS

Crested horn and Port Jackson sharks lay some of the most complicated and strange egg cases on the planet: a corkscrew-like package. Each of these bizarre screw-shaped cases contains one embryo. The odd design helps the egg case stay snug in rocks or coral while the tiny shark inside develops into a toothy predator.

CASSOWARIES

Prehistoric-looking cassowaries live in the dense tropical rainforests of Australia, Indonesia, and Papua New Guinea. From their electric blue heads and necks to their scarlet wattles and inky black feathers, these birds make quite an impression. So do their vibrant emerald eggs, colored to blend in with the ground where they build their nests.

BALANCING ACT

Acrobatic contortion is no longer relegated to dry land thanks to Tori Kubick, who's caused a sensation with her stand-up paddleboard routines.

Before discovering the wonders of stand-up paddleboarding, Tori enjoyed a career as a professional contortionist. Rigorously trained by a Mongolian contortion coach, she has added more balance exercises to her daily routine to support her work on the paddleboard. She remains constantly impressed by what the body is capable of with proper training and laser focus. And those observing her paddleboard routine are equally in awe of her physiology-defying moves.

CYCLE CLIMB

French mountain biker Aurélien Fontenoy "climbed" 33 floors on his bike without letting his feet touch the ground! The cyclist alternated between hopping and pedaling, taking just 30 minutes to ascend all 768 steps of Trinity Tower near Paris. His motivation behind the challenge? Raising money for a charity that helps care children dealing with serious illnesses.

AMERICA'S CUP
The America's Cup was first held in 1851, with yachts sailing 61 miles (98 km) around the Isle of Wight off the southern coast of England. The event was named after the winner of that inaugural race, a schooner known as *America*.

HARD CHEESE
Made from yak's milk, the Nepalese cheese chhurpi is as hard as a rock and needs to be softened before it can be eaten. Consequently, it is often chewed like gum for up to two hours.

CAP MOSAICS
Nina Krinitsina has spent over seven years decorating the exterior of her house in Makarye, Russia, with thousands of colorful plastic bottle caps. She has created more than 30 mosaics, mostly depicting characters from Russian cartoons and folk stories.

FAN FEED

TWO FOR ONE
Samuel Marshall sent us this anomaly he discovered while perusing his garden in Port Fairy, Victoria, Australia. It appears his green thumb was working overtime, as one of his dahlias decided to give him a two-for-one special with this stunning coloration split exactly down the middle of the bloom. In all actuality, it is likely a genetic phenomenon known as "codominance," in which two versions of the same characteristic (in this case, color) are inherited from both parents and expressed equally.

John Sevier Austin of Charlotte, North Carolina, can speak and sing backward! To show his talent, he films himself and then plays the video in reverse to reveal the actual words.

EAR PLUGS

Roosters tilt their heads back to crow in order to stop themselves going deaf from their own vocal sounds. This action covers their ear canal and serves as an ear plug. A rooster's crow typically reaches 100 decibels, making it as loud as a chainsaw.

WORD COUNT

English novelist Graham Greene was so disciplined he used to write exactly 500 words a day—even if it meant stopping in the middle of a sentence.

VETERAN DJ

Hong Kong DJ Ray Cordeiro retired in 2021 at age 96 after more than seven decades in radio. His popular radio show *All the Way with Ray* ran for 50 years.

BANKABLE DOLLS

Pebbles in *The Flintstones* was originally going to be a boy until the Ideal Toy Company said a girl would make more money because they would be able to sell Pebbles dolls. In just the first few months of sales, three million dolls were sold.

GRAPEFRUIT SPILL

A truck spilled its load of 1,000 grapefruits onto a busy highway in Ocoee, Florida, on December 11, 2019, bringing traffic to a halt.

GOLD BASS

Josh Rogers, of Bentonville, Arkansas, caught a one-in-a-million, gold-colored largemouth bass while fishing at Beaver Lake in the Ozark Highlands. Largemouth bass are usually shades of green and brown, but this fish's unusual coloring was due to a rare genetic condition called xanthochroism.

TEDDY BEAR

More than half of American adults still have their childhood teddy bear.

TINY BABY

When Pablo Picasso was born in 1881, he was so small and weak that the midwife thought he was stillborn and left him on a table while she attended to his mother. However, his uncle, a doctor, realized the baby was alive and saved him.

TREE NECKLACE

Aerial views of the Mei-ling Palace atop Xiaohong Hill in Nanjing, China, reveal unintentional tree growth resembling a giant necklace with a hanging emerald pendant.

A closer inspection reveals a road lined with large plane trees and a giant white palace with a green roof at the center of the so-called pendant. The effect gets heightened when the trees' leaves change color or when they get decorated with lights for nighttime displays.

BOUNCY BRIDGES

Seventeen bridges span the Ljubljanica River in Ljubljana, Slovenia, but nothing tops the two trampoline bridges that appeared in 2021!

Created by the Dunking Devils (DD) Squad, the trampoline bridges were the first of their kind. The narrower bridge invited spectators to get in on the bouncing. For two days, more than 5,000 people hopped across, logging more than 80,000 jumps. The second bridge contained professional trampolines on which the DD Squad, some of the planet's best freestyle trampoline athletes, performed gravity-defying feats during Bridge Bounce Ljubljana 2021.

STEAMPUNK SCULPTURES

Artist Peter Szucsy of Budapest, Hungary, crafts intricate steampunk sculptures out of parts taken from vintage cameras, medical equipment, watches, and other found objects.

Peter keeps about 300 vintage watches on hand to support his unique art form. Why so many timepieces? To collect enough of the same watch parts based on color, style, and material to make cohesive artworks. One of Peter's favorite subjects is spiders, but he's also created crabs and flies, with future ambitions of creating steampunk praying mantises and mosquitos.

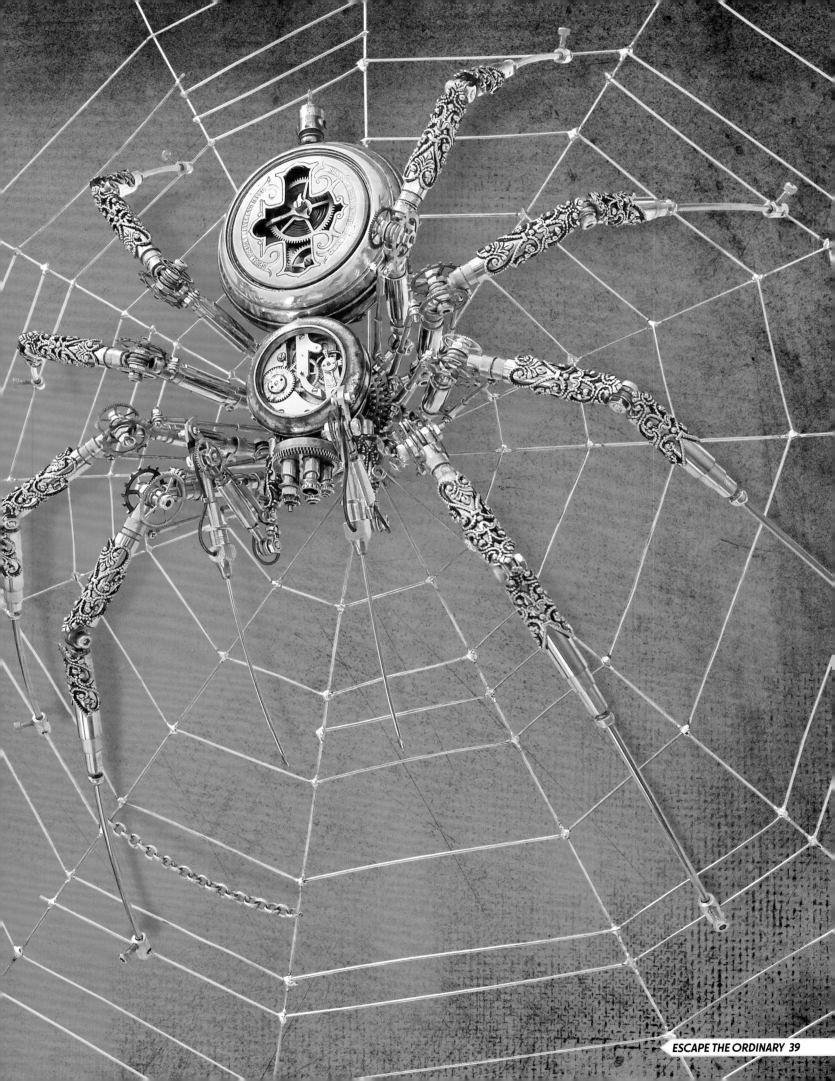

PRINTS PRANK

A next-level practical jokester, Tony Signorini of Clearwater, Florida, spent a decade making fake giant penguin footprints on local beaches and riverbanks.

In 1948, locals discovered the first set of prints, shocked by their vast size at 14 inches (35.6 cm) long and 11 inches (28 cm) wide. Although penguin-shaped, the faux footprints were hypothesized to come from a creature measuring 12 feet (3.7 m) long with massive flipper-like appendages. The paw prints eventually attracted the attention of Ivan Sanderson, a New York-based zoologist who came to Clearwater to investigate the cryptozoology mystery extensively. By 1958, Tony gave up the hoax, but he would wait another 30 years before revealing the truth about the immense penguin visitor.

PARROT ALARM

Anton Nguyen escaped from a late-night fire at his home in Brisbane, Australia, because his pet parrot, Eric, woke him by repeatedly squawking "Anton" to raise the alarm.

TREE RESCUE

Beverly McIntosh's female tabby cat Sparkles was stuck up a 60-foot-tall (18-m) tree in Jonesboro, Arkansas, for 18 days. After repeated attempts to lure her down with food failed, Sparkles was finally rescued by tree trimmer Clint Williams who climbed up the tree and plucked her from her lofty perch.

POISONOUS COAT

To give itself a poisonous coat to deter predators, the African crested rat licks deadly toxins into its own fur. The rat takes the toxins from the African poison arrow tree, which is often used to add deadly tips to arrows. The tree's poison is so lethal that just a few milligrams can kill a human, yet the rat is somehow immune.

HORROR MOVIE

A woman returned to her home in Torrance, California, on April 21, 2021, to find hundreds of birds flying around inside her house. The migratory swifts flew down the chimney before taking up residence.

PRIVATE CASTLE

Eccentric Spanish artist Salvador Dalí purchased a castle for his wife Gala in the late 1960s but would only visit her there if she sent him written permission beforehand.

GHOSTBUSTERS FAN

Robert O'Connor, of Elyria, Ohio, has collected more than 1,200 different items of *Ghostbusters* memorabilia, including signed LPs, production props, and action figures. He first saw the movie when he was four.

TRAINED PIGEONS

During World War II, American psychologist B. F. Skinner tried to teach pigeons to steer deadly missiles toward the enemy. When that failed, he successfully taught the birds to play table tennis instead. Skinner also taught his children's cats to play the piano.

DUNGEON MASTER

Robert Wardhaugh, of London, Ontario, Canada, has been playing the same game of the fantasy adventure *Dungeons & Dragons* for nearly 40 years. He began in 1982 with just four players; there are now about 60 people involved in the game and travel from all over Canada to play.

CRANE LANDING

The Japanese island of Kita Daitō is surrounded by coral reef cliffs, and the only way for most visitors to reach it is to be lifted through the air 33 feet (10 m) above the ocean in an elevator-like cage attached to a huge industrial crane.

LADYBUG LADY

Nadiia Komarova of Dnipro, Ukraine, owns more than 20,000 pieces of ladybug-related memorabilia. Items include handmade dolls, kitchen utensils, glass jars, salt and pepper containers, and more. Not only does she fill her house with these whimsical items, but she also wears red-and-black, insect-themed pieces, including pendants, bracelets, and scarves. No wonder a sign on the front door of her apartment reads, "Ladybug lives here."

BEAVER HAVOC
About 900 customers in Tumbler Ridge, British Columbia, Canada, lost their internet service when beavers chewed through an important fiber cable in several locations—even though it was protected by a 4.5-inch-thick (11.4-cm) conduit.

MANGO MAN
Horticulturalist Kaleem Ullah Khan, from Malihabad, India, has created a tree that produces 300 different varieties of mango.

FORGOTTEN SONG
The regent honeyeater bird from Australia has become critically endangered partly because it has forgotten its own mating song. The honeyeater used to be known for its complex song, but the males appear to have abandoned it and have started imitating other bird species instead, making it more difficult to attract females.

DISHWASHER NAP
After breaking in through a bathroom light, a raccoon trashed the kitchen of a home in North Ridgeville, Ohio, in March 2021 and was later found asleep in the dishwasher.

ONE-HANDED
Eleven-year-old Sankavi Rathan of Mississauga, Ontario, Canada, can solve 30 Rubik's Cubes one-handed while Hula-Hooping in about an hour. As she was born with a condition that gives her only limited mobility in her right hand, she solves the cubes left-handed.

OCEAN SIREN
Ocean Siren is a 13-foot-tall (4-m) sculpture situated above coral reefs off the coast of Queensland, Australia, that changes color in reaction to live water temperatures! The statue is a depiction of an indigenous girl named Takoda Johnson of the Wulgurukaba people and is the only part of the Museum of Underwater Art that can be seen above sea level. Created by British artist Jason deCaires Taylor, the sculpture features LED lighting powered by solar panels. The lights range from blue to dark red, based on water temperature readings, providing a visual warning of risks to coral reefs from warming seas.

WICKER MAN
Believe it or not, the burning of "Wicker Men" is not an ancient tradition but a relatively modern addition to festivals. Celebrated in Ireland, Beltane festivals are synonymous with the "Wicker Man," an effigy of wood and wicker burned at the height of revelries. The name "Beltane" refers to the Celtic deity of Bel and literally means "the fires of Bel." Traditional rituals include courting-related activities such as collecting flowers and lighting bonfires. But the addition of the festival's most recognizable symbol, the "Wicker Man," didn't happen until it was popularized by the films of the same name. Despite this, the modern tradition is still an incredible sight to behold and is likely to continue for many years to come.

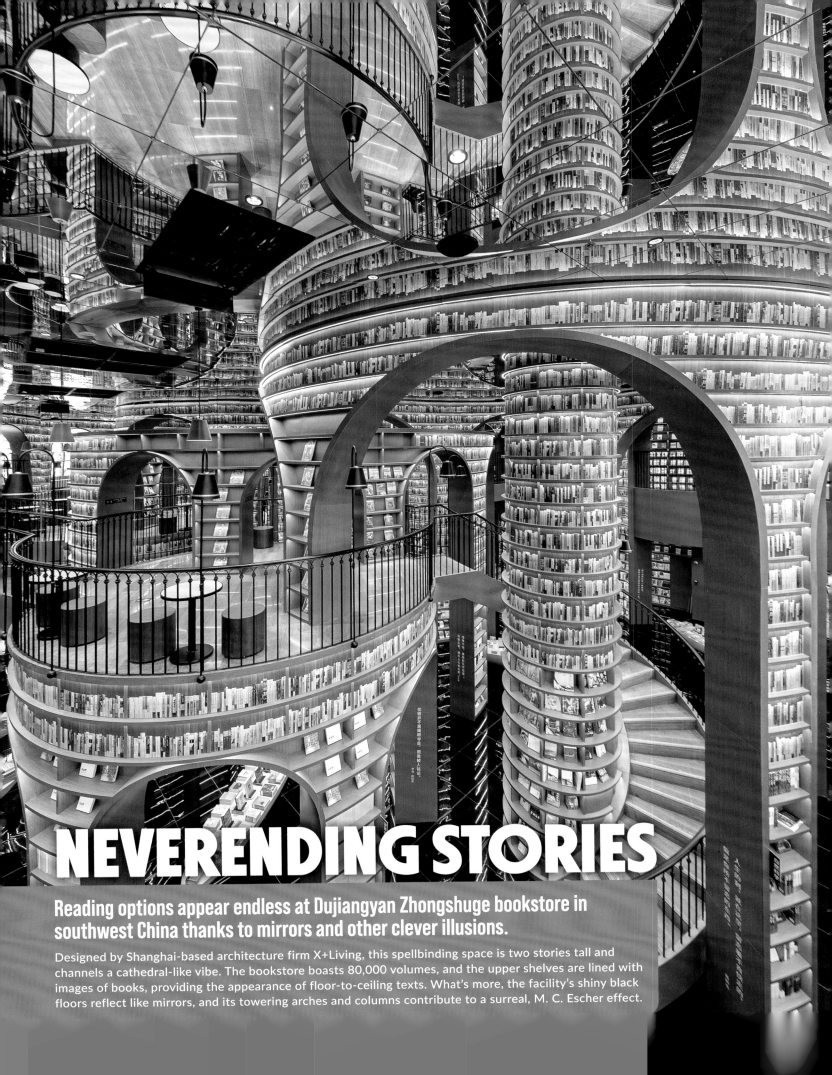

NEVERENDING STORIES

Reading options appear endless at Dujiangyan Zhongshuge bookstore in southwest China thanks to mirrors and other clever illusions.

Designed by Shanghai-based architecture firm X+Living, this spellbinding space is two stories tall and channels a cathedral-like vibe. The bookstore boasts 80,000 volumes, and the upper shelves are lined with images of books, providing the appearance of floor-to-ceiling texts. What's more, the facility's shiny black floors reflect like mirrors, and its towering arches and columns contribute to a surreal, M. C. Escher effect.

STRANGE MUSEUMS

Ripley's Odditoriums feature some of the strangest exhibits from around the world, but sometimes entire museums can be a Believe It or Not!

Some of the most famous museums focus on subjects like art, natural history, or science. But luckily for those with niche interests, there are institutions dedicated to just about any topic you can think of. In fact, there are more museums in the U.S. than there are Starbucks and McDonald's combined! This list is just a drop in the bucket of what you can find if you know where to look.

SPAM

The SPAM Museum in Austin, Minnesota, sheds light on everyone's favorite canned meat. Colorful displays celebrate this staple food and crowning achievement of food inventor Jay Hormel. And when questions arise, a SPAMbassador is never far away.

DOG COLLARS

The Dog Collar Museum at Leeds Castle in England contains more than 130 examples of rare and valuable canine neck accessories. The oldest piece in the collection dates to the fifteenth century and protected a mastiff from attacks by bears and wolves. These age-old dog collars will make you rethink the history of man's best friend.

BARBED WIRE

The Devil's Rope Museum in McLean, Texas, pays homage to barbed wire, an artifact that helped "win the West." Exhibits include more than 2,000 samples of the fencing material along with other frontier pieces fundamental to America's ranching heritage. A variety of historical research materials, photos, and barbed wire sculptures are also on-site.

TOILET SEAT ART

A city in Texas known as The Colony is home to Barney Smith's Toilet Seat Art Museum. This one-of-a-kind location is the brainchild of none other than Barney Smith, a former plumber who naturally gravitated to the seats as a creative outlet. The artist crafted more than 1,400 masterpieces using these porcelain throne covers, some of which include historic artifacts like pieces of the Berlin Wall.

POO

England's National Poo Museum on the Isle of Wight sits in an impressive Victorian fort, Sandown Barrack Battery, atop scenic coastal cliffs. Despite the posh home, the museum focuses on excrement. From lion poop to human feces, samples are preserved and displayed in resin spheres. Curators hope their exhibits will take some of the taboo out of products of a necessary function.

RAMEN

Located on the bottom two levels of Japan's Shin-Yokohama Ramen Museum, "Ramen Town," is a replica of an urban Japanese neighborhood in the late 1950s. But there's more to the museum than just aesthetics. Ramen Town contains nine real restaurants where you can sample diverse regional noodle styles.

MAD MAX 2

The Mad Max 2 Museum in Silverton, Australia, represents a veritable shrine to one of sci-fi's most iconic dystopian creations, the *Mad Max*-verse. Created by Adrian Bennett in 2010, he chose Silverton because filmmakers used it as a location for the movies. There, you'll find full-size costumes, working replica cars, and an impressive photography collection.

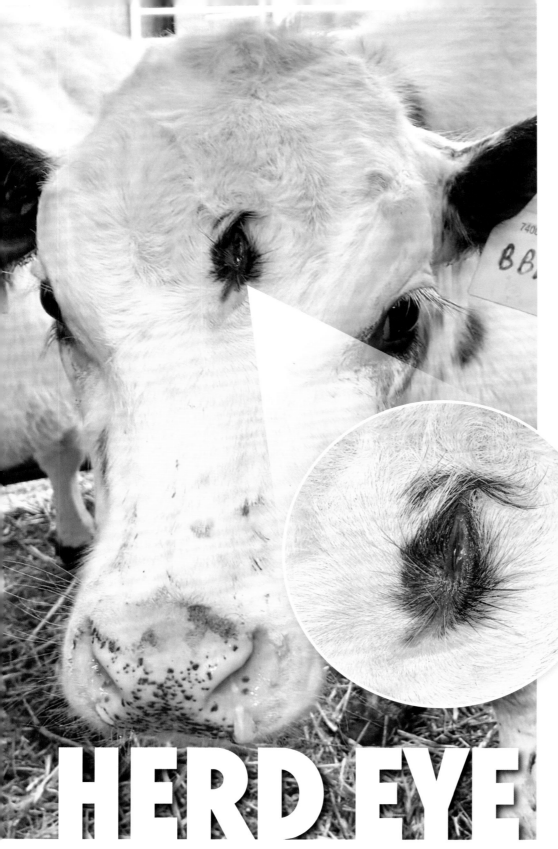

HERD EYE

A calf in Wales had everyone seeing triple after they noticed it was born with a third eye directly in the middle of its forehead!

Veterinarian Malan Hughes was conducting a tuberculosis test on the baby bovine, then four months old, when she noticed the extra eye. The calf appeared healthy, with Malan noting that the third eye seems functional although misplaced. It has eyelids and eyelashes, and it even secretes lubricant, keeping it moist. However, it is not known whether the calf can use it for sight.

REGURGITATED GOAT

Mr. Yao, a farmer in Quanzhou, China, found a 13-foot-long (4-m) python regurgitating his missing 88-pound (40-kg) goat after having swallowed the animal whole. The snake spent an hour vomiting up the dead goat, helped by villagers who constantly pulled the snake's tail and massaged its stomach.

TOO HAPPY

Rolo, a dachshund owned by Emma Smith from Essex, England, was so happy to have his owner around all the time after she started working from home that he sprained his tail from wagging it too much.

FAITHFUL FRIEND

A loyal dog spent more than 18 months waiting at a roadside shrine near Nafpaktos, Greece, where his owner, Haris Korosis, had died in a traffic accident. From time to time, local people tried to adopt the dog, but he kept returning to the same spot.

SENSITIVE SNOUT

The 22 tentacle-like protrusions on the snout of the star-nosed mole are six times more sensitive than a human hand, allowing it to feel its way around the dark underground tunnels where it lives.

MUTANT GOAT

In April 2020, a goat with two faces was born at Jocelyn Nueske's farm in Wittenberg, Wisconsin. The goat, which had two mouths, two noses, and four eyes and ate with both heads, was named Janus after the two-headed Roman god.

PROSTHETIC WINGS

To enable it to fly properly, a green-cheeked parakeet named Wei Wei was fitted with a pair of prosthetic wings by veterinarian Dr. Catherine Apuli in Brisbane, Australia. The prosthetics were made of feathers that had been donated to the clinic.

SHARP SCALES

The skin of the elephant trunk snake, which lives in rivers in Southeast Asia, is covered with small, sharp scales that it digs into its victim to prevent escape.

BEACH WORMS

Thousands of fat innkeeper worms, some 1 foot (0.3 m) long, washed up on Drakes Beach in Northern California in December 2019. Storms in the area had forced the worms out of their underground burrows and dumped them on the beach.

CUB RESCUE

A pet dog turned up at its owner's home in Washington County, Virginia, with a three-week-old black bear cub in its mouth. It is thought the dog had rescued the orphaned cub and gently carried it home. The cub was unhurt and was fostered out to a female bear.

AGILITY ABILITY

An adorable Boston Terrier named Gus defies the odds by competing in agility competitions despite losing his eyesight. He lost one eye after a collision with a tree, and the other succumbed to infection shortly after. Although he is totally blind, Gus spends his weekends flyball and agility training, relying on his owner's commands to jump and navigate obstacles.

PEPPER HOME

While chopping vegetables at their home in Saguenay, Quebec, Canada, Nicole Gagnon and Gérard Blackburn found a tree frog living inside a fully intact green bell pepper.

OCEAN RESCUE

When her owner Lance Schloss's boat was capsized by huge waves during the night in Moreton Bay, Queensland, Australia, Heidi the German shepherd dog treaded water for 11 hours in the ocean before a fisherman spotted her. Her presence alerted rescuers to 63-year-old Mr. Schloss, who was also eventually saved after spending 15 hours in the freezing water clinging to the upturned boat. He credited Heidi with saving his life.

SHOPPING TRIP

Self-isolating at home in Mexico during the coronavirus outbreak, hungry Antonio Muñoz sent his pet chihuahua, Chokis, to a nearby shop to buy some Cheetos—with a note and money attached to its collar.

TOWEL SNACK

Veterinarians in Sydney, Australia, safely removed an entire beach towel from the stomach of an 18-year-old female carpet python named Monty by pulling the towel out very slowly through the snake's mouth.

SCARED SHARKS

Great white sharks are so afraid of killer whales that they will avoid an area for up to a year after spotting one.

AUTO POLO

From "horseless carriage" to "horsepower," car lingo still pays homage to its four-legged predecessors. But did you know that auto polo was once a thing? In the early twentieth century, Ford Model Ts attempted to replace steeds on the polo field with mixed results. Each car had a driver and a mallet man who clung to the side of the vehicle, attempting to hit a basketball. Games kept spectators on their toes, reportedly reaching speeds of 40 mph (64 kmph) and involving hairpin turns and flipped cars.

KNIFE-THROWING GRANNY
Galina Chuvina, from Sasovo, Russia, did not take up knife throwing until she was 56 but went on to become eight-time Russian national champion, European champion, and even world champion in the sport. The knife-throwing granny was presented with a new meat grinder when she won her first competition, and when she went on to claim the national title, she was presented with a cell phone and an air mattress.

PRESIDENTIAL SANDWICH
Steve Jenne, from Sullivan, Illinois, has kept a sandwich half-eaten by Richard Nixon for more than 60 years. Jenne was a 14-year-old Boy Scout when Nixon visited Sullivan in 1960 during his presidential campaign. Nixon ate half of a buffalo barbecue sandwich, and Jenne took the other half and has kept it in a freezer ever since. He also stores unfinished foods from entertainers Tiny Tim and Henny Youngman.

POPCORN DUMMER
German musician and robotics engineer Moritz Simon Geist invented a drum kit that is played not by a human drummer but by popcorn. A frying pan is filled with popcorn kernels and hot oil, and each time a kernel pops, it sets off a series of sensors located above the pan. These in turn trigger a connection to the drums and cymbals.

LAUGHTER EPIDEMIC
In 1962, an epidemic of laughing broke out in a school near Kashasha, Tanganyika (modern-day Tanzania), affecting 95 of the 159 students aged between 12 and 18, but none of the teachers. Symptoms lasted from a few hours to 16 days, and over the next 18 months, it spread to other schools in the region before suddenly dying off. In total, 14 schools were shut down and 1,000 people were affected.

LONG SENTENCE
Convicted of defrauding more than 16,000 people, Chamoy Thipyaso was sentenced to 141,078 years in prison in Thailand in 1989. She was released after serving only eight years.

RING RETURNED
Melisse De La Mare lost her platinum wedding ring in 1992 while skiing at Mount Bachelor in Bend, Oregon—and it turned up 27 years later 2,400 miles (3,840 km) away in Bessemer, Alabama. A customer told Alabama jewelry maker Heather Langley about a ring he had found while working a summer job at Mount Bachelor in the early 1990s, and Langley used the inscription inside the band to trace De La Mare and return the ring to her.

GOLDEN TOILET
In 2019, thieves stole a $6 million golden toilet from Blenheim Palace in Oxfordshire, England, the birthplace of Winston Churchill.

ROLLER RACE

Every year, the city of New Orleans hosts a Running of the Bulls–inspired race featuring roller derby skaters instead of cattle!

Rather than risk being gored by angry bulls bent on destruction in the streets of Pamplona, Spain, participants of the "N'awlins" event get chased by a fleet of roller derby girls wearing horns and wielding giant plastic bats. The Spanish-inspired chase begins and ends at The Sugar Mill event venue, and along the route you'll have plenty of opportunities to run for your life or risk a clobbering from bovine-channeling queens of the rink.

HEAVY LIFTING

Battulga Battogtokh, a.k.a. Tulga, of Chicago, Illinois, has earned a reputation for incredible feats of strength, including balancing a 100-pound (45-kg) flaming, twirling log atop a metal implement held in his mouth. Incredibly, he is even able to hang from circus aerial straps while the log is suspended from a contraption held by his tightly clenched teeth. Tulga's astonishing escapades have taken him all over the world, including Australia, France, Germany, Italy, and Russia.

BARBIE NEST

A weaver bird in Johannesburg, South Africa, added a Barbie doll to its nest. The doll had been thrown onto the roof of a home by a young boy, and two days later it reappeared in the nest 6.5 feet (2 m) away, with the doll's hair woven into the structure.

BACK TO WORK

Linda Oswald's two-year-old border collie–red heeler mix, Tilly, went missing after being ejected through the shattered rear window of the family's car when it was involved in an accident on Idaho State Highway 41—but two days later he was found herding sheep on a farm at Rathdrum 1.5 miles (2.4 km) away.

WALKS UNDERWATER

The chevrotain, or mouse deer, can escape predators by diving into a river or stream and walking along the bottom. It is able to hold its breath underwater for up to four minutes.

FREE RIDE

Lauren Russell's two-year-old golden retriever, Wally, gave a woodchuck a ride to shore on his back after the two animals met while swimming in Hickory Hills Lake in Lunenburg, Massachusetts. The rodent climbed onto the dog's back and stayed there during the 330-foot (100-m) swim to dry land before the new friends said goodbye to each other with a gentle nuzzle of their noses.

ANT NAPS

Worker ants take around 250 naps every day, but each nap lasts only a minute.

CHESS PRODIGY

By age 10, Frederick Waldhausen Gordon, from Edinburgh, Scotland, had already beaten a Grandmaster at chess. He started playing when he was only six, and within a week he was defeating his parents, both of whom have PhDs in math.

TOP CAT

Over a period of nine months, Floki the cat summited 48 of New Hampshire's tallest mountains—including the 6,288-foot-high (1,917-m) Mount Washington—while riding in her owner Mel Elam's backpack.

HEROIC RAT

Magawa, an African giant pouched rat, was trained to sniff out land mines in Cambodia, and over a five-year period the rat identified more than 100 mines and other explosives, thus saving countless human lives. Magawa was awarded a PDSA gold medal for animal bravery—an honor previously reserved for dogs.

MINIATURE BUILDINGS

Using everyday objects like wooden coffee stirrers, cardstock paper, barbecue skewers, plastic bottle caps, and toothpicks, Tracy Ealdama handcrafts miniature models of iconic stores, diners, and other businesses in Toronto, Canada.

RAPID READER

Maria Teresa Calderon from the Philippines can read up to 80,000 words a minute with 100 percent comprehension. The average person reads about 250 words per minute with 70 percent comprehension. At university she read a three-page, 3,135-word, college-level essay in just 3.5 seconds.

Located on Extraterrestrial Highway in Alamo, Nevada, the Black Mailbox is a designated hotspot for passersby to drop letters addressed to aliens.

HOBBIT LIFE

Pastry chef Nicolas Gentile has spent the last few years leading the life of a hobbit in a diminutive home situated in the Italian countryside.

Besides hanging out at the "Shire," he mixes it up with peers dressed as Aragorn, Legolas, Gimli, and the rest of the fellowship from *The Lord of the Rings*. In perhaps his most audacious feat, Nicolas and a Tolkien-inspired crew embarked on a 180-mile (290-km) trek to Mount Vesuvius. Not one to miss an opportunity to emulate Frodo, Nicolas brought along a replica of the One Ring, which he lobbed into the crater. Good riddance!

Ripley's Exhibit
Cat. No. 22487

FIRST-CLASS FORK

A first-class fork emblazoned with the White Star Line logo. The *Titanic* was one of White Star Line's passenger ships. Believe it or not, the last meal enjoyed by the first-class passengers on the *Titanic* was an extravagant 10-course dinner.

Ripley's Exhibit
Cat. No. 167326

MATCHSTICK *TITANIC*

A 1:115 scale model of the ill-fated RMS *Titanic*. Tim Elkins of West Sussex, England, used 147,000 matchsticks to complete the impressive copy. Believe it or not, only three of the ship's iconic smokestacks actually worked! The builders thought four looked more impressive.

RMS TITANIC
AUTHENTIC ANTHRACITE
FROM THE 1912 MAIDEN VOYAGE
RIPLEY'S BELIEVE IT OR NOT

‹ Ripley's Exhibit
Cat. No. 18402

RECOVERED COAL

This is one of several coal pieces recovered from the wreckage of the *Titanic* since it was rediscovered in 1985. Believe it or not, it took 600 tons of coal per day to keep the *Titanic* running—all of which had to be shoveled into furnaces by hand around the clock.

NO FINGERPRINTS

For several generations, the men in the Sarker family from Rajshahi, Bangladesh, have had no fingerprints—the result of a very rare genetic condition called adermatoglyphia. They were born with completely smooth fingertips, meaning that some of the family have been unable to obtain a driver's license.

OPEN GRAVE

Radboud University in the Dutch city of Nijmegen dug an open grave so that students could lie in it to relieve exam stress.

POULTRY IN MOTION

A 42-year-old man from Milwaukee, Wisconsin, was arrested for drunk driving while having a live chicken perched on his left shoulder.

HANGING CONTEST

In the sport of *gaffelhangen*, popular in the Limburg area of the Netherlands, competitors have to hang for as long as possible onto a pitchfork suspended from a metal frame without falling to the ground.

MARRIED BRIEFCASE

Rain Gordon, from Moscow, Russia, is attracted to inanimate objects, and in 2020 she "married" Gideon, a metallic briefcase, in an unofficial wedding ceremony that was attended by family and friends. She had bought Gideon from a hardware store in 2015 as a prop for a photoshoot and later dumped a human boyfriend in favor of the briefcase, to which she felt a stronger emotional connection.

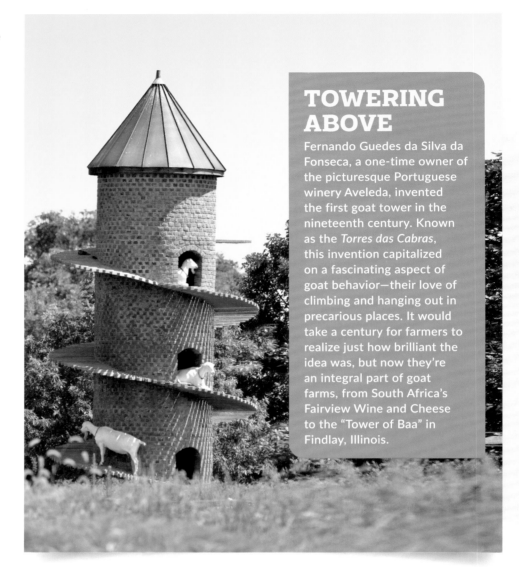

TOWERING ABOVE

Fernando Guedes da Silva da Fonseca, a one-time owner of the picturesque Portuguese winery Aveleda, invented the first goat tower in the nineteenth century. Known as the *Torres das Cabras*, this invention capitalized on a fascinating aspect of goat behavior—their love of climbing and hanging out in precarious places. It would take a century for farmers to realize just how brilliant the idea was, but now they're an integral part of goat farms, from South Africa's Fairview Wine and Cheese to the "Tower of Baa" in Findlay, Illinois.

TWO-TONED

A rare genetic mutation has resulted in a stunningly beautiful and incredibly rare pink-and-green grasshopper. Photographed by Calvin Taylor Lee of Yorkshire, England, who found the insect in a grassy meadow hiding behind a stalk. The tiny grasshopper's rose-colored torso and long green wings make it more vulnerable to predation from birds. Yet, it appeared fully grown, making it not only pretty but lucky!

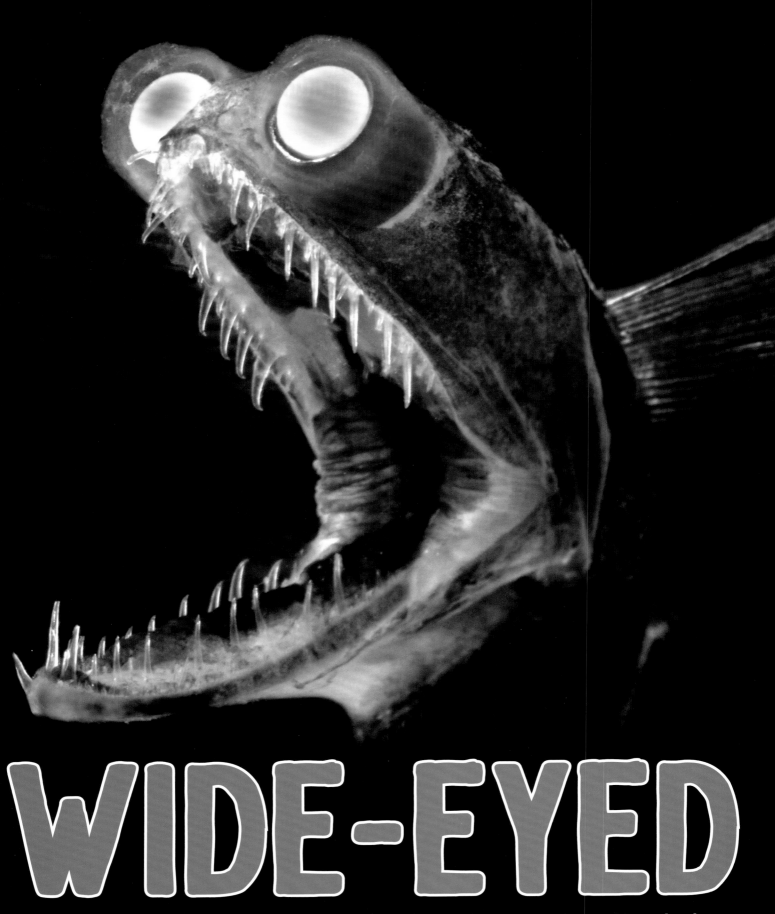

WIDE-EYED

Deep-sea telescopefish have eyes that look like a pair of large, translucent binoculars!

Scientists believe these strange-looking eyes help the telescopefish find bioluminescent creatures—animals that create their own light—to eat. Another clue that points to the mysterious fish's glowing grub is the black tissue that lines its stomach. It's thought that this dark matter is used to conceal the glow of the animals they consume!

MASSIVE

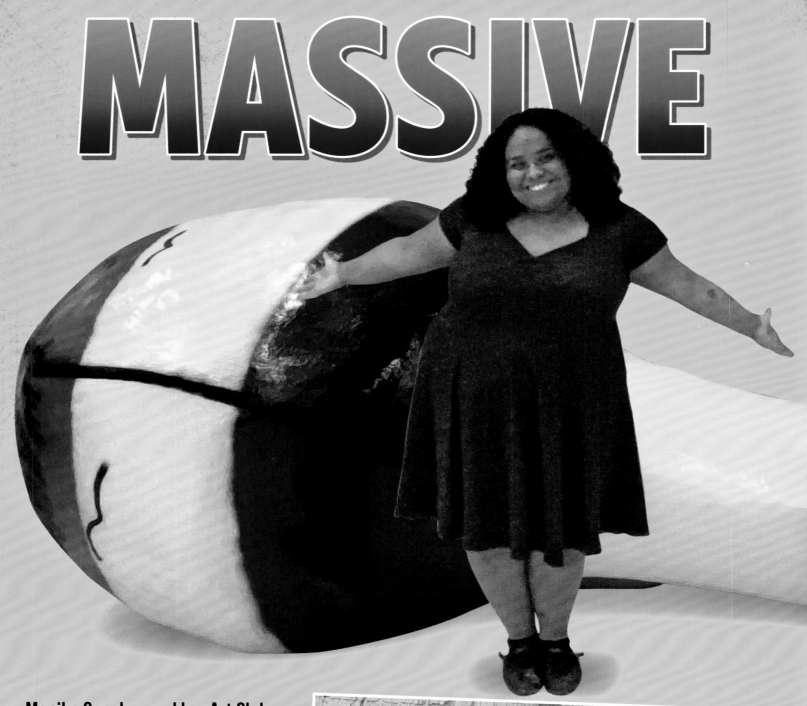

Monika Sanchez and her Art Club students at United South Middle School in Laredo, Texas, crafted giant papier-mâché maracas!

The immense instruments measure a whopping 13 feet (4 m) long and 4 feet (1.2 m) tall. This wasn't Monika's first foray into colossal crafts; some of her previous pieces include a 6-foot-wide (1.8-m) concha, a.k.a. Mexican sweet bread, and a giant cascaron egg complete with confetti! She collaborated with her students on the maracas as a way of "shaking off the negative energy." As Monika notes, the papier-mâché sculptures represent "a symbol of pride in both culture and creation." Monika and the USMS Art Club look forward to undertaking more enormous projects in the future.

MARACAS

13 FEET (4 M) LONG AND 4 FEET (1.2 M) TALL

ALL SMILES

Every fall, a 300-foot-wide (91-m) smiley face appears on a forest-covered hillside between Willamina and Grand Ronde, Oregon. It was created by using two different types of conifer trees, with the face forming as one species changes color in the fall. The eyes and mouth are made up of Douglas fir, which remains green all year round, and the rest of the face is composed of larch, the needles of which turn yellow as winter approaches. Planted in 2011 by Hampton Lumber, the face is expected to last another 30 to 50 years.

STRANDED TOURISTS

Baunei, a mountain village on the Italian island of Sardinia, attempted to ban the use of Google Maps in 2019 after there were 144 reported cases of tourists getting lost. Fire service and rescue teams were regularly needed to help stranded visitors to the area who had followed directions on the app.

HELPFUL LABEL

Two men were arrested in Pensacola, Florida, while carrying a bag full of drugs with the words "Bag Full of Drugs" written on it. Ian Simmons and Joshua Reinhardt, both from Orlando, had been pulled over for speeding, and the incriminating bag was found in the car.

ALCOHOL PEE

A 61-year-old woman in the United States became the first person in the world to be diagnosed with urinary auto-brewery syndrome, a condition that causes her to pee alcohol—even though she doesn't drink. Doctors in Pittsburgh, Pennsylvania, detected that yeast in her bladder ferments the abnormally high levels of sugar in her urine to produce alcohol.

NEXT-LEVEL FILTER

Invented in the late 1930s by Semyon and Valentina Kirlian, Kirlian photography, a.k.a. electrophotography, captures images of corona discharges, like haloes or energy fields, around objects and subjects. For many years, people claimed that this glow captured is the "aura" of a living creature. However, it is actually the ionization of fluid or gas surrounding an object. When the same method of capturing these images is attempted in a vacuum, it does not work!

FLIGHTS OF FANCY

In 1876, Alexander Graham Bell changed the world by patenting the first telephone, but many people forget he also dabbled in aerodynamics with tetrahedral kites.

The Scottish-born Bell got the idea for these aviation marvels after watching box kites fly. A tetrahedron is a pyramid with four sides; Bell thought the shape could be the key to unlocking flight. By utilizing three-dimensional prisms with four sides, he could increase the weight-to-surface area ratio of each kite. The largest kite Bell successfully flew included 3,393 cells and could carry a human passenger!

SPIRIT PHOTOGRAPHY

Spirit photography was all the rage in the late nineteenth and early twentieth centuries, but while this photographic trend gained an ardent following, it also inspired the ire of critics like P. T. Barnum, who claimed these photos preyed on grieving families.

William Mumler, an American amateur photographer, launched spirit photography in the early 1860s when he "caught" an image of his dead cousin on film. Because his photographic career coincided with the Civil War, the images he crafted appealed to Americans turning to spiritualism to communicate with loved ones lost in battle.

Soon, other photographers followed in his footsteps, forging thriving businesses. How did they get away with the fake photos? People struggled to debunk them. Photography was still in its infancy, and few were familiar with the double exposure technique used to superimpose ghostly images atop those of living people.

WHIMZEYLAND

Florida artists Todd Ramquist and Kiaralinda have spent the past 20 years transforming their home in Safety Harbor into Whimzeyland, a psychedelic explosion of brightly painted recycled art.

Initially, Todd and Kiaralinda referred to their home simply as the "Bowling Ball House," but they soon realized the flamboyantly decorated joint deserved a name upgrade. Whimzeyland was born. Besides featuring approximately 500 painted bowling balls, you'll see crafted colored-bottle gardens, vibrant ceramic sculptures, and rainbow-hued mosaic pathways. The result is an eye-popping experience people drive from all over the nation to tour.

BAR BUCKS

After Martin and Molly McGuire opened McGuire's Pub in Pensacola, Florida, in 1977, people got into the habit of decorating the walls with signed dollar bills. Today, nearly every inch of the 15,000-square-foot (1,394-sq-m) establishment is covered in the "green wallpaper," translating into $2 million worth of cash. In 1996, the couple opened a second location in Destin, also plastered in autographed dollar bills.

✉ FAN FEED

SPY TOOTH

Tampa, Florida, dentist Dr. Michael Foley has transformed 007-style fiction into reality by crafting an assortment of spy-inspired secret agent teeth. Constructed from real human molars, each tooth contains a hollow chamber with a realistic false crown. A pin and hinge mechanism made from nickel-titanium release the crown. The result? A mini compartment perfect for storing documents and microfilm—but not cyanide. (Most experts agree this last "Hollywood" fiction is too dangerous for reality.)

KGB Spy Tooth allegedly used to hide suicide cyanide pill

FEAR FACTOR

An irrational fear, or phobia, is different from a simple dislike or aversion in that it causes extreme distress.

Phobias often originate from traumatic experiences, so while some may seem silly, the anxiety they produce is very real. Common phobias include arachnophobia (fear of spiders) and claustrophobia (fear of enclosed spaces), but here are some you probably aren't familiar with.

PHOBOPHOBIA

As the name suggests, phobophobia is the fear of phobias. Described as "free-floating anxiety," think of it as the fear of fear itself. Individuals suffering from this disorder often avoid situations that produce anxiety, and the condition usually coexists with other phobias.

ARACHIBUTYROPHOBIA

How do you feel about getting peanut butter stuck to the roof of your mouth? For those with arachibutyrophobia, this scenario sounds intolerable. The origins of this phobia may include everything from fear of choking to a peanut allergy. Whatever the case, it drives people to avoid the sticky stuff like the plague.

HIPPOPOTOMONSTROSESQUIPPEDALIOPHOBIA

Ironically, the fear of long words holds the record for being the longest word in the English dictionary. Known as hippopotomonstrosesquippedaliophobia, it refers specifically to the embarrassment that comes with having to pronounce long words aloud.

DEIPNOPHOBIA

Most people dislike eating alone at a restaurant or even at home. But for a small percentage of the population, dining in front of others leads to anxiety. This phobia, known as deipnophobia, leaves individuals feeling awkward when chowing down around others and may stem from overly strict etiquette rules in childhood.

CHAETOPHOBIA

Chaetophobia involves the fear of hair and may stem from a traumatic experience associated with a person's tresses, whether a bad haircut or going bald. Others feel terror at the sight of a hairball on the ground, perceiving others' locks as dirty and something to avoid touching.

EISOPTROPHOBIA

People who fear mirrors and other reflective surfaces have a phobia known as eisoptrophobia. While most people associate mirror avoidance with vampires, you don't have to be a bloodsucking member of the undead to find looking glasses repugnant. Causes for the condition vary from low self-esteem to fear of bad luck or seeing a ghost on the reflective surface.

GLOBOPHOBIA

Some people fear clowns, a condition is known as coulrophobia. But those with globophobia dread what clowns are frequently seen carrying: balloons. Just the sight of one of these gas-filled spheres can trigger extreme anxiety, making events like birthday parties challenging.

FLYING SHIP

Spectators did a double take after seeing what appeared to be a cruise ship floating above the surface of the sea, the result of a "superior" mirage caused by temperature inversion. This optical illusion, also known as a "fata morgana," occurs when warm air sits atop a layer of cold air, causing the light coming off the ship to bend, creating a blended color effect.

BRIGHT BLOCKS

The Comfort Town housing complex in Kyiv, Ukraine, looks like a LEGO city that has been brought to life! The colorful, geometric neighborhood is situated on 115 acres (46.5 hectares) and includes everything from housing to shopping, schools, and restaurants. Its vibrant colors were chosen to provide a stunning contrast to the neighboring gray buildings.

MACABRE FESTIVAL

At the annual Carnevale festival in Lula, Sardinia, the victim—or *battileddu*—is dressed in parts of a freshly slaughtered cow or goat, wearing the animal's horns as his own, its stomach lining as a hat, and its still steaming heart as a belt buckle. He is driven through the town by men carrying real bullwhips who sometimes also lash out at onlookers, even drawing blood.

To create a snack in honor of National Ice Cream Sandwich Day on August 2, 2019, Oscar Mayer introduced a hot dog ice cream sandwich, putting real chunks of meat into ice cream.

HISTORIC COURSE

Golfers are not allowed to use modern equipment at the historic Oakhurst Links in White Sulphur Springs, West Virginia. Instead, they dress in period clothes and use nineteenth-century hickory-shafted clubs and gutta-percha balls that are driven from a small pile of sand as was the custom before wooden tees were invented.

DIFFERENT LANGUAGES

In the farming village of Ubang, Nigeria, men and women speak separate languages. Boys are raised speaking the women's version of the local dialect until they reach the age of 10 when they are expected to switch to the men's language, where many of the words are completely different.

STUPA SOLUTION

Sonam Wangchuk, a scientist and engineer from Ladakh, India, has started creating artificial glaciers to help combat water shortages.

To create these icy towers, a pipe is buried into a water source high up on a mountain; the rest of the pipe goes down the peak to where the water is needed, usually farmland. The water flows downhill through the pipe, creating enough pressure for it to blast out of a tall vertical tube at the bottom. The water falls to the ground and freezes into a two-story mound called an "ice stupa." During the summer months, when water is scarce, the melting stupa creates a new source of life-giving liquid.

PAINTING WITH POO

German artist Werner Härtl creates intricate paintings celebrating Bavaria's rural heritage while using a surprising medium: cow dung!

Despite the strange "paint," Werner's monochromatic artworks resemble sepia photographs, rich in detail. He first happened upon the idea of using cow dung as a medium while working as a farmhand. After collecting and bringing home a container of liquid cow dung, he experimented with using it on various surfaces, including watercolor paper, canvases, metal, wood, and plastic. Soon, he started crafting incredible artwork portraying some of Germany's most beautiful pastoral and agricultural landscapes. Intrigued by his work, Ripley's asked Werner a few burning questions about his paintings.

Q. Of course, we must ask: Do your paintings smell like cow manure?
A. When it is wet, the "paint" is a bit funky. But when it's completely dry, it doesn't smell anymore.

Q. What steps do you take to turn the fresh "material" into paint?
A. Well, I fetch the cows' droppings with a canister as soon as they lift their tails. Around two bowel movements deliver enough for half a year of creativity. While painting, I use water to dilute the dung and achieve different shades. I start scribbling using very dry, gentle brushstrokes. Then, I use watered-down dung for light shades. Finally, I use dung with no water mixed in for the dark shades.

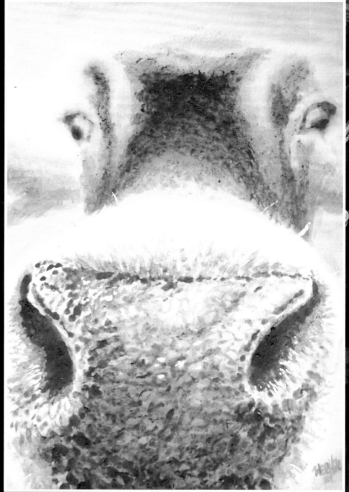

Q. Is cow dung always the same color, or is there a variety? Does it change depending on the cow or what they eat?

A. As with all digesting organisms, the color of feces depends on the health of the individual and on the food, but since a cow's food goes through multiple stomach chambers, the final outcome is pretty similar.

Q. What do you wish more people knew about your art?

A. Humor is a big part of my work, but working with dung has a serious purpose. I want people to rethink our view on the environment: what we rely on, which resources we claim for everyday life. Are rural landscapes—including nature, culture, traditions—just scenery to look at, simply a matter of aesthetics?

People tend to think a pleasant life should be all clean, stylish, entertaining, and convenient. But without the "dirt" everything grows out from, without working in sweat, without knowledge gained from failure, none of the above would be enjoyable.

Q. How long do your paintings last? Do you preserve them in any way?

A. Paintings on canvas are finished with varnish. That way the colors stay intense, and the movement of the canvas doesn't make the dry dung fall off. The oldest dung painting I have is about 12 years old, and it still has its brilliance. But to this day, I experiment with the effects weather, especially the sun's, has on the paintings.

"When it is wet, the 'paint' is a bit funky. But when it's completely dry, it doesn't smell anymore."

TOUGH BEETLE

The diabolical ironclad beetle of North America has a shell so strong it can withstand being run over by a car. Although the beetle is only 0.8 inches (2 cm) long, its protective exoskeleton allows it to resist a force 39,000 times its body weight. That is equivalent to an adult human withstanding the weight of 280 double-decker buses.

OWL COPILOT

An owl boarded an airborne helicopter that was helping to fight the Creek Fire in California in October 2020. The bird flew in through the window of pilot Dan Alpiner's helicopter and perched quietly inside while he was mid-flight conducting water drops before leaving the same way it had arrived.

UNEXPECTED VISITOR

After a herd of about 40 cows escaped from a farm in Victoria, Australia, one was found sitting on a trampoline in the garden of Kay Laing's home in nearby South Gippsland. The cow needed help to get off the trampoline because it was unable to stand up on the bouncy surface.

BOTH SEXES

A research team at the Powdermill Nature Reserve in Rector, Pennsylvania, discovered an extremely rare rose-breasted goshawk that was half male and half female. The bird had male plumage on one half of its body and female coloration on the other—a condition known as "bilateral gynandromorphy."

PAPER BIRDS

When Pastor Kazuhiro Sekino, a Japanese chaplain at Abbott Northwestern Hospital in Minneapolis, Minnesota, appealed for paper cranes with which to decorate the hospital in 2020, he expected to receive around 200. Instead, an staggering 16,000 origami birds were sent to him from all over the world!

LANDSLIDE SURVIVOR

A dog in Guizhou Province, China, was found alive and well after spending 37 days trapped under the rubble of destroyed buildings following a massive landslide in 2020. The whole of Cangbaotian village was evacuated, and only a handful of its 130 buildings were left standing. But over a month later, Chen Yongen returned to see what was left of his collapsed home and heard barking from beneath the debris. It was his dog, and 12 villagers then spent 10 hours digging the animal out.

SOLO VOYAGE

Lisa Blair sailed counterclockwise around the entire coast of Australia nonstop and unassisted in 58 days. Starting and finishing in Sydney Harbor, she covered 7,521 miles (12,104 km). In 2017, she had become the first woman to circumnavigate Antarctica solo in a sailboat.

POKING AROUND

Aye-ayes of Madagascar are about 2 feet (0.6 m) long including their tails and have developed an incredible adaptation known as "percussive foraging" using their skeletal middle fingers. These fingers have an astonishing range of motion due to their ball-and-socket joints. Aye-ayes use them to search for wood-boring grubs by tapping on branches and then pulling the grubs out. Sadly, perhaps because of their eerie appearance and nocturnal nature, some people consider aye-ayes bad luck and kill them on sight.

CREEPY FINGER!

SOLE FOOD

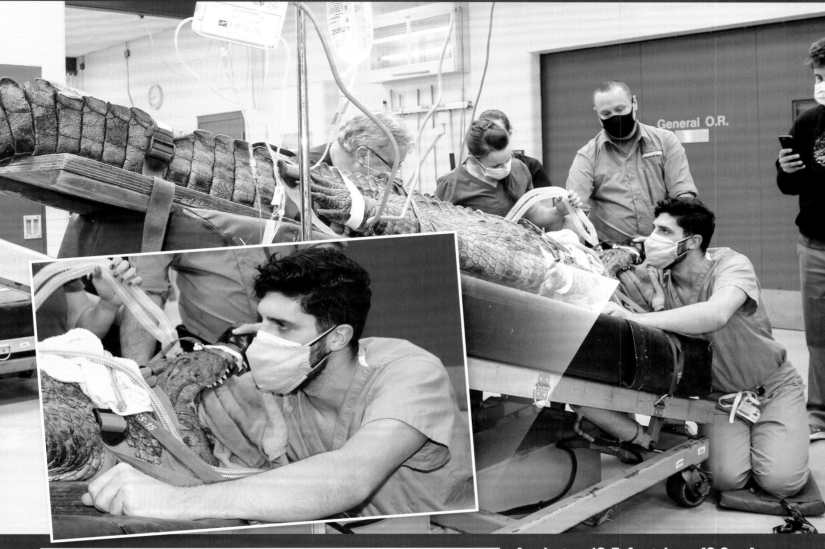

Anuket, a 10.5-foot-long (3.2-m), 341-pound (155-kg) crocodile who lives at St. Augustine Zoological Park in Florida required surgery to remove a shoe from her stomach.

Anuket devoured the empty shoe after it slipped from the foot of a visitor ziplining above the reptile's enclosure. She then regurgitated the footwear and ate it a second time! Zoo medicine resident Garrett Fraess at the University of Florida College of Veterinary Medicine attempted to retrieve the shoe by sticking his arm down the (sedated) reptile's mouth, but it was too far gone. It was ultimately removed in surgery by Dr. Adam Biedrzycki. Anuket is now back home and healthy!

Believe it or not, the shoe is now in the Ripley's collection and can be seen at our Odditorium in St. Augustine, Florida!

TURTLE CALL
Baby sea turtles call to each other while they are still in their eggshells so that they can all hatch at approximately the same time.

SNAKE SCARE
Trish Wilcher was shocked to discover 18 nonvenomous snakes—17 baby snakes and their mother—under her bed in her home in Augusta, Georgia.

FAST FINGERS
Using only one hand, Japan's Kazuya Amitani pulled 172 facial tissues out of a box one at a time in 60 seconds—equal to nearly three tissues a second.

PLANE SPOTTER
Six-year-old Aarna Gupta, from Panchkula, India, can identify 93 different airlines in one minute by looking at the planes' tails.

GOLF HAZARD
While playing golf at the Spring Island Club in Okatie, South Carolina, on April 5, 2021, David Ksieniewicz saw his ball land on the back of a sunbathing, 7-foot-long (2.1-m) alligator. Wisely, he decided the ball was unplayable, allowing the alligator to waddle into a nearby lake with the ball still in place on its back.

LONG LASH
On the upper eyelid of her left eye, You Jianxia, from Shanghai, China, has an eyelash that is an incredible 8 inches (20 cm) long.

YOUNG DESIGNER
U.S. fashion designer Michael Kors worked on his first project—redesigning his mother's wedding dress for her second marriage—when he was only five years old.

Playing cricket in West Yorkshire, England, in June 2021, Asif Ali hit the ball right out of the field and through the windshield of his own car that was parked nearby!

DEEP HOLE
Seventy-six-year-old Dona Geralda was trapped in a 10-foot-deep (3-m) hole in Curvelo, Brazil, for eight days but survived by drinking rainwater. She fell in a remote woodland area where nobody heard her cries for help. She was eventually found clinging desperately to a vine in the rain-filled hole.

LONG TONGUE
A pangolin's long, sticky tongue can stretch up to 16 inches (40 cm) and enables it to eat 70 million ants and termites a year. In some species of pangolin, its fully extended tongue can be longer than its body.

ELBOW DRAG
U.S. professional motorcycle racer Josh Herrin reached a speed of 101 mph (162 kmph) on a motorbike while dragging his elbow along the ground for 100 feet (31 m) at Buttonwillow Raceway Park, California.

FLYING KISS
Chongqing, China's "Flying Kiss" attraction features gigantic sculptures of a man and a woman who pick up passengers on the ground and then lift them into the air, turning toward each other for what looks like a kiss. In the process, riders gain 360-degree panoramic views while overlooking a 3,000-foot (914-m) cliff, with no seatbelts, seats, or safety harnesses attached. In other words, one misstep could transform the "Flying Kiss" into the "Kiss of Death."

FLESH
FASHION

Artist and DJ Doooo from Kawasaki, Japan, creates accessories and gadgets that bear a striking, and somewhat disturbing, resemblance to human body parts.

One of his pieces that's garnered the most attention is a coin purse shaped like a mouth and chin, whose fleshy lips you can move and jaw you can open to deposit change into. Besides the quirky wallet, Doooo has also made an iPhone case covered with what looks like human skin, a dice cube with an eye that realistically blinks, and a finger-shaped flesh—uh, flash drive. He uses resin and silicone to create each masterpiece and sells them through his store, MOTHER FACTORY.

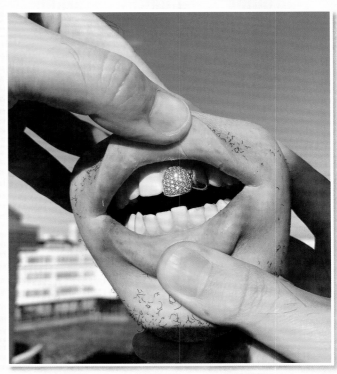

Ripley's Exhibit
Cat. No. 170837

BURMESE MARIONETTE

For hundreds of years, puppet shows were the most popular form of entertainment in the country of Myanmar (formerly Burma). Members of the country's royal monarchy frequently attended the plays, further increasing their cultural importance. A traditional Burmese marionette troupe consists of about 28 characters, each with a specific role to fill.

INDONESIAN SHADOW PUPPET

This flat wooden doll is actually a puppet once used in shadow performances called "wayang." Wayang theater originated on the Indonesian island of Java more than a thousand years ago! The puppets and puppeteer are separated from the audience with a thin screen. Lit from behind, the figures' shadows are projected onto the screen.

KONGO POWER FIGURES

Seen here are examples of power figures called "nkisi," made by the Kongo people who live along the east coast of Central Africa. The human-shaped one is called a "nkisi nkondi," while the dog is known as a "kozo." The small statues were used in community ceremonies, with each nail serving as a record of agreements, treaties, and disputes.

MADE OF SUGAR!

PERFECT PETALS

Most sugar flower artists struggle with the challenge of making their work appear lifelike, but award-winning confectioner Michelle Nguyen has the opposite problem. She crafts such realistic flora that you'd be hard-pressed to convince somebody to take a bite. How does she pull off the look? By studying the movements and colors of leaves and petals with incredible attention to detail. Among her favorite flowers to create are peonies and dahlias.

LIFTED CAR

For a short period of time, people walking along a quaint street in the Odenwaldkreis district in Germany came across an unlikely sight: half an emerald-green Ford Granada protruding from the side of Matthias Hoffmann's house. Mounted on two supports, the car appeared to rest effortlessly from the house's façade. But keeping it there was harder than its designers imagined—it turns out the building is a recognized cultural monument, and country officials ordered the car to come down due to potential damage to the house.

MATCHSTICK BAND

Ukrainian artist Bogdan Senchukov makes life-size, playable musical instruments—including guitars, accordions, violins, and drums—from matchsticks. He spent six months and used 27,000 matchsticks to build a bass musical instrument in the shape of a trident, the Ukrainian coat of arms. He and his friends perform in their very own matchstick band, playing 15 of his matchstick instruments.

GREAT ESCAPE

The *Regimbartia attenuata* water beetle can survive being eaten by a frog. The insect slides down the amphibian's throat, swims through its stomach and intestines, and finally climbs out of the frog's rear. It usually takes several hours for the beetles to escape, but some have completed the journey in only six minutes.

JOSH-OFF

In a mock battle dreamed up by Arizona student Josh Swain, hundreds of people with the first name Josh dressed in costumes and took part in a fight with foam pool noodles at Air Park, Nebraska, to decide the "rightful owner" of the name. The crowning champion was four-year-old Josh Vinson, Jr.

NEON SIGNS

Chicago art school graduate Percy Lam has recreated more than 100 of Hong Kong's iconic neon signs by hand embroidery. He replicates the city's bright restaurant and hotel signs with variously colored stitches on small sheets of black paper. Each embroidered artwork can take him up to seven hours to complete.

TATTED TEACHER

Sylvain Helaine (a.k.a. Freaky Hoody) is the most tattooed man in France, having spent approximately 460 hours under the needle getting his body, face, tongue, and even the whites of his eyes inked.

In a fascinating twist of fate, he's also a primary school teacher on a mission. You see, Sylvaine believes his unusual appearance teaches students a vital lesson about not judging a book by its cover. Teaching children from the age of six and up, he notes that the first day of school comes with an initial shock. But once students and their parents get to know the art-covered fellow, it's business as usual.

FLOATING STONES

In the wintertime, rocks and large stones seem to magically float above the water on Siberia's Lake Baikal. The phenomenon, which is known as "Baikal Zen," is caused by strong winds whipping across the lake and around big stones to carve out pedestals of ice that protrude above the lake's frozen surface. These gravity-defying stones are left balancing precariously on the thin pillars of ice, but from a distance they appear to be floating in midair.

1,100-POUND (499-KG) SANDAL!

SIZEABLE SHOES

At Tokyo's Sensoji Temple, you'll find an enormous pair of straw sandals, or owaraji, measuring 14.5 feet (4.3 m) tall and weighing a whopping 1,100 pounds (499 kg) each. Their human-sized counterparts, made from straw ropes, were all the rage up until the nineteenth century. But why the colossal pair? First introduced in 1941, locals meticulously craft a new replacement pair every decade to scare off evil spirits and demons by evoking Niō, the muscle-bound giant guardians of Buddhist temples.

SHOE POLISH

Elvis Presley was born with sandy blond hair, but in his teens, he started coloring it black with shoe polish as a cheap alternative to hair dye to make himself look edgier.

WHEELCHAIR FIGHT

For one episode of the 1950s TV action series *The Adventures of William Tell*, actor Conrad Phillips played the legendary Swiss folk hero from a wheelchair after breaking his foot in a fall. Even Tell's fighting scenes were done from a wheelchair.

STRING PORTRAITS

Artist Ben Koracevic, from London, England, creates portraits of celebrities, movie characters, and animals using only black string and thousands of nails carefully positioned on a blank white canvas. His version of Dwayne "The Rock" Johnson required 6,000 nails and 3,936 feet (1,200 m) of string, and took 250 hours to complete. His artworks sell for up to $5,000.

BEE SUIT

For an episode of the TV show *Malcolm in the Middle*, actor Bryan Cranston wore a suit of more than 10,000 live bees for an hour—but was stung only once.

HANGING OUT

There are cemeteries suspended from cliffs in Sagada, the Philippines, put there by indigenous people following ancient traditions.

The practice dates back thousands of years but is no longer prevalent, with burials on the cliffs only taking place once every few years. Some coffins are noticeably shorter; this is because it was once common practice to fold the deceased into the fetal position—sometimes breaking bones in the process—since it was believed the body should leave this world as it entered it. The body is then wrapped tightly in fabric, carried up the mountain, and placed in its coffin. No one is completely sure why the practice began. One belief is that the cemeteries served to place the bodies closer to their ancestral spirits, while others think they provided a creative way to keep bodies out of the waterlogged soil.

FUNGUS AMONG US

Huitlacoche is a fungus that causes corn kernels to swell with monstrous, mushroom-like structures—a much sought-after Mexican delicacy. This multicellular fungus puts off many spores and has a bluish-gray and white appearance. Huitlacoche contains complex flavors, ranging from earthy to sweet, pungent to savory. This treat dates back to the Aztecs, who relied on huitlacoche as a vital foodstuff.

HAT TRADITION

On St. Catherine's Day in France, unmarried 25-year-old women (called "Catherinettes") are presented with outrageous green and yellow hats, often made for them by friends, which they must wear all day.

CITY CRUSH

If the 7.8 billion people of the world stood shoulder to shoulder, they could all fit within the 500 square miles (1,300 sq km) of Los Angeles.

PERFECT TIME

Jens Olsen's World Clock in Copenhagen, Denmark, has 15,448 working parts and took him 27 years to build. As long as it is wound once a week, it is designed to keep perfect time for thousands of years.

WHISTLING LANGUAGE

The language Silbo Gomero has no spoken words, only whistles. It is a form of a Spanish dialect, with vowels or consonants replaced by a whistling sound of varying pitch and length. The 22,000 inhabitants of La Gomera in the Canary Islands use the language and can communicate with each other from several miles away.

PAPER NAPKINS

Eygló Ingólfsdottir, from the island of Heimaey, Iceland, has a collection of 14,000 paper napkins dating back to 1955. Her napkins, some of which depict Disney characters and Santa Claus, even survived the 1973 volcanic eruption that forced her family to evacuate the island for three years.

DUMPSTER DISCOVERY

While converting a mill into a wine bar in 1999, Andy Clynes, a builder from Oldham, England, stumbled across more than $10,000 worth of design drawings by Paul McCartney in a dumpster. The drawings were for the "magic piano" that was used in the Beatles' 1967 film *Magical Mystery Tour*.

 FAN FEED

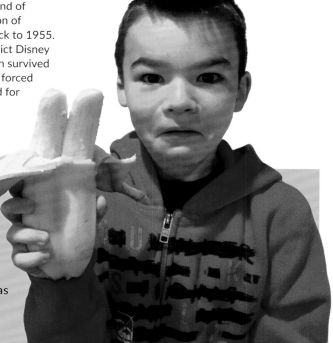

A-PEEL-ING FIND

Paxson Courtnay of Anchorage, Alaska, shared his strange find with us: two bananas in one peel! The fruit was part of a normal bunch of bananas brought home from the grocery store, but a closer inspection revealed an extra-wide specimen. You can see Paxon's surprise upon peeling the anomaly! Luckily, two-for-one bananas like this are perfectly safe to eat.

FLOWER FLOATS

Every spring, the town of Bad Aussee, Austria, hosts a festival celebrating the wild-growing daffodils that blanket the meadows of Traun Valley.

The main event of the Daffodil Festival is the boat parade. Participants craft a frame in the shape of their subject, cover it in netting, and then insert thousands of colorful daffodil blossoms. Up to 300,000 flowers might be used for a single float! The themes are often inspired by fairy tales, animals, and pop culture. Once complete, these elaborate figures are towed along the picturesque waters of Lake Grundlsee, where hundreds of people gather on the shore to take in the views.

GOOD TO BE KING

When viewed from above, the Salisbury Plain of South Georgia Island in Antarctica appears to be covered by flowing rivers of white and brown, but a closer look reveals thousands of penguins!

Standing about 3 feet (0.9 m) tall, king penguins are the world's second-largest penguin species after the emperor penguin. Known for forming enormous colonies, the group at Salisbury Plain contains hundreds of thousands of individuals. Despite this reproductive success, most king penguins take two full years to raise a single chick. Interestingly, their fluffy brown chicks were once mistaken as a distinct species and dubbed the "woolly penguin" by scientists.

SUNKEN CITY

The Deep Dive Dubai pool in the United Arab Emirates holds 3.7 million gallons (14 million liters) of freshwater—the equivalent of six Olympic-sized swimming pools—and even contains an underwater city!

The 196-foot-deep (60-m) pool contains cutting-edge sound and lighting systems, plus 56 cameras to ensure divers' safety as they explore abandoned apartments and even search for treasure. In case of emergency, the facility boasts a highly advanced hyperbaric chamber. Should you visit Deep Dive Dubai, make sure you don't follow up with a trip to the world's tallest building (also in Dubai). As a sign at the pool points out: "After any dive, it's recommended to wait 18–24 hours before ascending higher than 300 meters (1,000 feet)."

REEL WORLD

Located in the picturesque countryside of Aberdeenshire, Scotland, you'll find the Lochter Fishery, which includes a leaping-trout-shaped lake. Known as the Muckle Troot Loch, fishery workers keep it stocked with the finest quality rainbow trout, drawing fishing fanatics from all over the world.

GARDEN WALK

To raise money for Britain's National Health Service, 99-year-old army veteran Captain Tom Moore completed 100 laps of his garden in Bedfordshire, England, with the help of a walker. Each lap measured around 82 feet (25 m). For his 100th birthday a few weeks later on April 30, 2020, he was made an honorary colonel, reached number one on the UK singles chart with his cover of "You'll Never Walk Alone," and received more than 125,000 birthday cards!

RARE PROTOTYPE

An ultra-rare Nintendo PlayStation prototype—the product of a short-lived collaboration in 1992 between Nintendo and Sony—sold in 2020 for $360,000. The project was scrapped before the console was ever released, and the unit sold at auction is thought to be the only one not destroyed.

PRETZEL SHAPE

It's said the pretzel was invented in 610 AD by an Italian monk who, to reward children for learning their prayers, folded the strips of bread dough so that they looked like the crossed arms of people praying.

FLOATING STUDIO

Rock musician Dave Gilmour recorded parts of the last three Pink Floyd studio albums aboard the *Astoria*, his houseboat studio moored on the River Thames in Surrey, England. The boat, which can accommodate a 90-piece orchestra on its top deck, was built in 1911 for British music hall impresario Fred Karno, the pioneer of the slapstick pie-in-the-face gag beloved by comedy acts such as Laurel and Hardy and The Three Stooges.

CHICKEN BONE

A 22-year-old woman who complained of a long-lasting cough was found to have had a piece of chicken bone lodged in her lung for 14 years. A bronchoscopy performed by doctors in Guangzhou, China, revealed the presence of the 0.8-inch-long (2-cm) bone.

APOSTROPHE SOCIETY

Retired journalist John Richards, from Lincolnshire, England, ran the Apostrophe Protection Society for 18 years before closing it down in 2019 at age 96 because he felt that fewer people cared about punctuation and the correct use of the apostrophe in the English language.

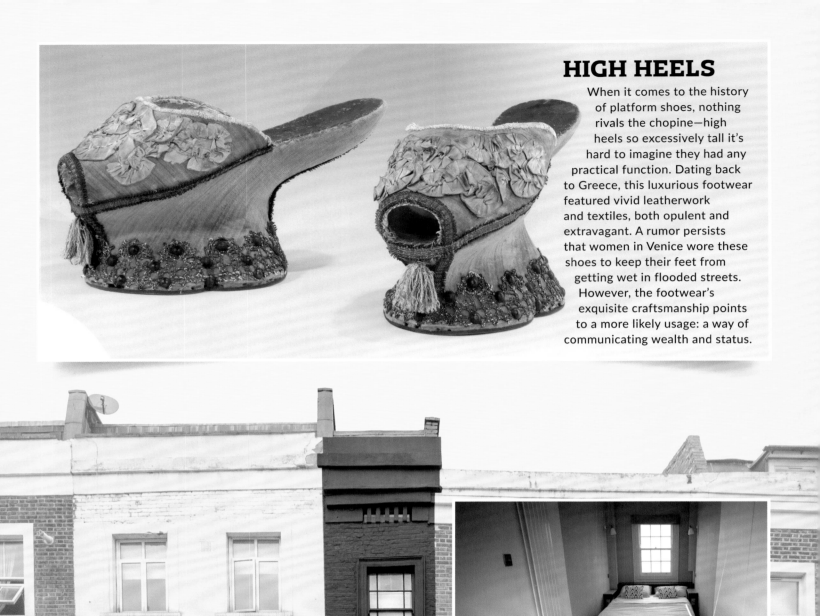

HIGH HEELS

When it comes to the history of platform shoes, nothing rivals the chopine—high heels so excessively tall it's hard to imagine they had any practical function. Dating back to Greece, this luxurious footwear featured vivid leatherwork and textiles, both opulent and extravagant. A rumor persists that women in Venice wore these shoes to keep their feet from getting wet in flooded streets. However, the footwear's exquisite craftsmanship points to a more likely usage: a way of communicating wealth and status.

NARROW LIVING

This home in London measures just 6 feet (1.8 m) wide in most places! The widest point of the house falls just under 10 feet (3 m), and while most "tiny homes" have less than 400 square feet (37 sq m) of living space, this house has 1,034 square feet (96 sq m) thanks to its five floors, which include a landscaped garden, two bedrooms, and a rooftop terrace. Before being transformed into a living space, the house was originally a hat shop.

BODY HACKING

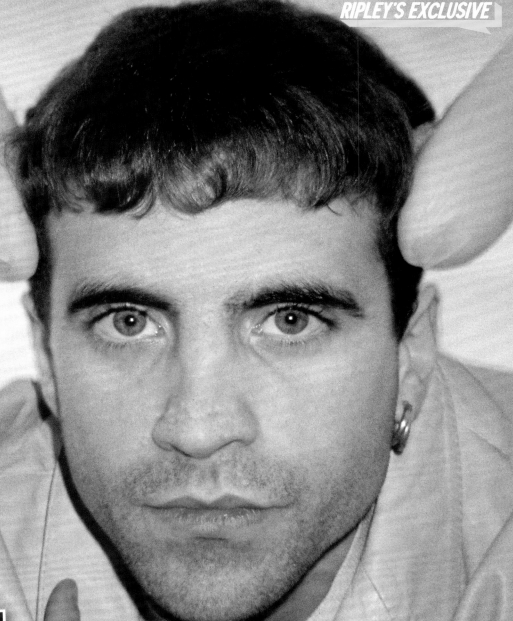

Spanish cyborg artist Manel de Aguas has a pair of fish-inspired fins surgically implanted in his head that enable him to hear the weather!

His Weather Fins, which resemble large white seashells, have been inserted on both sides of his head above his ears and are attached to the temporal bones in his skull. They are connected to his brain through circuits and serve as functional organs that allow him to detect changes in temperature, humidity, and atmospheric pressure. They also send sound waves to his brain through bone conduction. The fins can be recharged with solar energy and connect to devices via Wi-Fi.

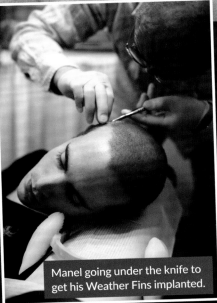

Manel going under the knife to get his Weather Fins implanted.

Q. What inspired the design of the Weather Fins?
A. The design of the Weather Fins is divided in two different paths: the "sense" design and the "organ" design. The sense design is the stimuli I perceive, which was inspired by underwater sounds, and allows me to experience the atmosphere as if I'm submerged in a sea. The organ design—the shape of the body part—was inspired by the fins of flying fish.

Q. How long did it take to get used to the Fins?
A. It took me around a month to get used to the new stimuli and a bit more to get used to having a new physical body part.

Q. What does it feel like when the Fins are giving you information?
A. It feels as if I am submerged in a liquid environment that is constantly changing its properties.

Q. What are some unexpected benefits of the Weather Fins?
A. They have increased my empathy toward nature and all other non-human species.

VOLATILE VOLCANOES

Volcanic eruptions have both fascinated and terrified human beings for millennia.

Despite vast leaps in volcanology over the past few decades, we still have a long way to go in understanding and predicting these geologic time bombs. Nevertheless, it's hard not to marvel at the sheer force of these sublime natural features. These are some of the most extreme eruptions in recorded history.

Krakatoa. Rep. Roy. Soc. Com.

Plate 1.

View of Krakatoa during the Earlier Stage of the Eruption from a Photograph taken on Sunday the 27th of May, 1883.

NOVARUPTA

The record for the largest volcanic eruption of the twentieth century and beyond goes to Novarupta in Alaska, which blew on June 6, 1912. Novarupta spewed 30 times more lava than Mount St. Helens and shot ash 19 miles (30.5 km) into the sky. Remarkably, there were no known human deaths. Today, a 1.2-mile-wide (2-km) lava dome marks the volcano's vent.

KRAKATOA

The eruption of Krakatoa on the Indonesian island of Rakata produced the loudest sound in recorded history. People reported hearing it 3,000 miles (4,828 km) away, describing it as "cannon fire from a nearby ship." Over the next five days, the pressure wave created by the sound of the volcanic event circled the planet seven times.

MOUNT ST. HELENS

Washington's Mount St. Helens erupted in 1980, releasing 24 megatons of thermal energy. The blast was so powerful it blew off about 1,300 feet (396 m) of the mountain's peak, leaving a massive crater. It also leveled all of the trees within 6.2 miles (10 km), thousands of which are still floating in the nearby Spirit Lake today.

BEFORE

AFTER

LAKI

Over the course of eight months, Iceland's Laki eruption of 1783–84 spewed 42 billion tons of basalt magma and toxic gases. These gases contaminated the soil, killing half of the country's livestock and most crops. Lava flattened 21 villages, and 69 percent of residents died. Temperatures dropped globally due to the sulfur dioxide the volcano released, causing crop failures in Europe, North Africa, and India.

MOUNT PELÉE

One of the deadliest eruptions in history occurred on May 7, 1902, in the Caribbean at Martinique's Mount Pelée. When the volcano exploded, it released a 1,000°F (538°C) pressure wave that demolished every structure in St. Pierre and instantaneously killed up to 40,000 people. Reportedly, one of the handful of survivors included an alleged murderer, who was saved by his stone prison cell.

MOUNT VESUVIUS

When Italy's Mount Vesuvius erupted in 79 AD, the scalding ash fell so quickly onto the city of Pompeii that it virtually vaporized everyone within. When the ruins were discovered more than 1,600 years later, archaeologists poured cement into the hollow molds left behind in the ash, revealing human forms that bear a silent, somber witness to victims' final moments.

MOUNT TAMBORA

In April 1815, the largest explosive eruption in recorded history occurred at Mount Tambora. Located on Indonesia's Sumbawa Island, the volcano whipped up pyroclastic flows and tsunamis, killing at least 100,000 islanders and leaving another 35,000 homeless. The blast removed more than 3,000 feet (914 m) of the mountain's height and left it with a 3.7-mile-wide (6-km), 3,609-foot-deep (1,100-m) caldera.

FINE ART FAWN

Michigan multimedia artist Chris Roberts-Antieau turns old taxidermy into masterpieces by adding detailed embroidery on fine French netting. In the piece *Albino Deer*, she covered the creature with plants and animals native to the deer's natural environment that it would have seen while alive. To create the intricate patterns, Chris sketches a detailed drawing of her vision; then she creates patches that are applied to a fine netting, which she sews by hand to fit the animal. She has used this technique to transform other old taxidermy, including deer heads, a bear, a swan, and a full-body hyena.

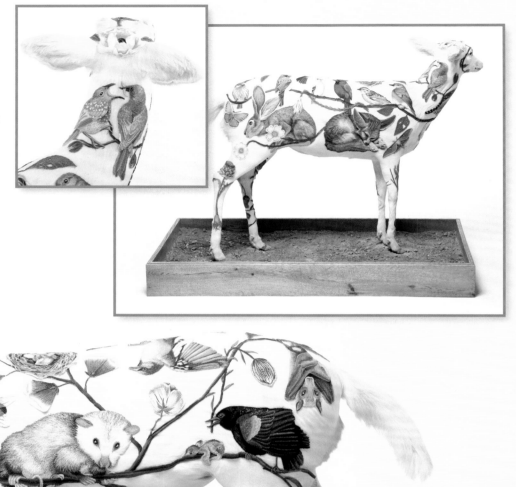

VIKING SHIP

After spending two and a half years and thousands of dollars using cardboard and 50 pounds (23 kg) of hot glue to build a 16-foot-tall (5-m) and 30-foot-long (9-m) replica Viking ship at Rogersville, Missouri, artist Kyle Scheele celebrated the completion of the project by deliberately burning it to the ground as a form of traditional Viking funeral.

DENTAL CARE

Although it is now considered to be bad for your teeth, machine-spun cotton candy was co-invented under the name "fairy floss" by an American dentist, William Morrison, in 1897. Then in 1921, another dentist, Joseph Lascaux from New Orleans, came up with a new machine for making the sugar confection and renamed the product "cotton candy."

ANCIENT GUM

By sequencing the DNA from a piece of 5,700-year-old chewing gum found in southern Denmark, researchers were able to discover that the chewer was a female with dark skin, dark hair, and blue eyes. The Stone Age gum was made from birch pitch, a substance formed by burning the bark of a birch tree.

SKELETON SKILLS

Artist Laurel Cunningham-Hill combines her love of nature and the morbid by crafting delicate jewelry and unique art pieces out of rodent bones found inside owl pellets.

Painstakingly dissecting each plug of regurgitated bone and hair with the precision of a surgeon, she upcycles this natural "waste" into decorative wristwatches, earrings, broaches, and intricate framed pieces that she refers to as Capsulariums. From a skeletal couple holding hands to a devil stag crowned with five horns, her masterpieces bridge the gulf between captivating and creepy.

MADE OUT OF RODENT BONES!

ROCKY NO HANDS

Rocky Stoutenburgh of Southgate, Michigan, was left paralyzed from the neck down after an accident in 2006, but today he plays video games professionally using only his mouth!

How does one play games without the use of their hands? With a device called the QuadStick, a mouth-based video game controller developed specifically for quadriplegics. At his brother's suggestion, Rocky began streaming himself playing battle royale games in 2016. Now he has more than 70,000 followers on Twitch, where he goes by RockyNoHands, and he is the first quadriplegic gamer to join a professional esports organization! Rocky's accomplishments have encouraged other people with disabilities and brought awareness to the need of accessibility in gaming.

To use the QuadStick, Rocky uses head movements, presses a button with his lips, and sips or blows air into holes to play games like *Call of Duty: Modern Warfare* and *PUBG: Battlegrounds*.

BODY LASSO

Brown tree snakes in Guam have learned to turn their bodies into lassos in order to be able to climb up tall, smooth, metal cylinders and reach bird boxes at the top.

LONG DROP

Female giraffes give birth standing up, meaning that newborns arrive with a 5-foot (1.5-m) drop to the ground. Even so, baby giraffes are able to stand within 30 minutes of being born.

CHALK SCULPTOR

Indian artist Sachin Sanghe sculpts detailed portraits of celebrities and images of Hindu gods into sticks of chalk. He has completed more than 200 chalk miniatures, including a tiny replica of the Taj Mahal that took him 80 hours. He started carving chalk in high school using geometry tools such as dividers, a compass, a sharpener, and safety pins.

SKUNK ODOR

The smell of a skunk is so strong that a human can detect it up to 1 mile (1.6 km) away.

NEW BODY

A species of Japanese sea slug can sever its head and soon grow a whole new body, including a new heart. When it first sheds its body, the slug lives on as just the head for three weeks, even though it has no vital organs.

POOH BEAR-BNB

Few fictional characters are as relatable as Winnie the Pooh, who wants nothing more than to spend quality time with his friends and enjoy a tasty snack. In September 2021, fans of the silly old bear could embrace their inner-Pooh with a stay in the "Bearbnb" at Ashdown Forest in East Sussex, England. The woodlands served as author A. A. Milne's inspiration for the Hundred Acre Wood, home of Pooh Bear and his friends. The Bearbnb itself was based on Pooh's tree house and was filled with references to the nearly 100-year-old story, including "hunny" pots and wallpaper drawn by Kim Raymond, who has illustrated Winnie the Pooh for more than 30 years.

EXPLODING DYE PACK

This radio-controlled bank security pack is made from 100 real $20 bills. Packs like these are hidden alongside real money in banks. If triggered—such as in the case of a bank robbery—the pack explodes, getting permanent dye all over the stolen bills and sometimes the thief, helping officials track down the criminal.

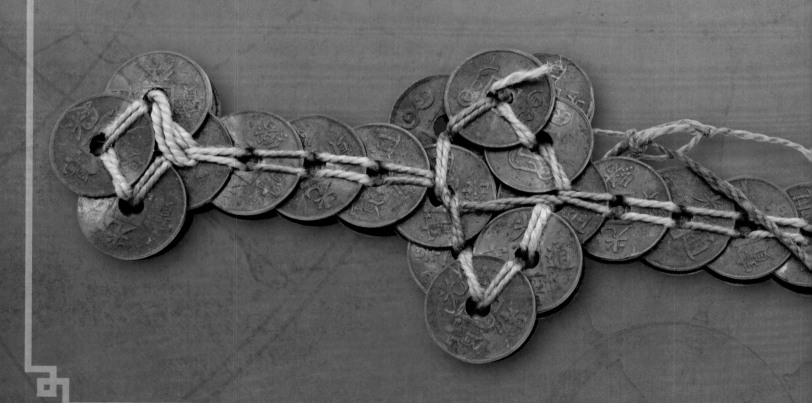

Ripley's Exhibit
Cat. No. 175019

100-TRILLION DOLLAR BILL

One of the largest money denominations ever printed is the 100-trillion Zimbabwean dollar bill. Despite the large number, they weren't worth much when they were circulated in 2009 due to hyperinflation. One bill could barely buy a loaf of bread. The bill has since been discontinued and is now more valuable as a collector's item.

REAL "CASH" SWORD!

Ripley's Exhibit
Cat. No. 7499

COIN-SWORD

On a physical level, coin-swords are exactly what they sound like—coins strung together in the shape of a sword. Chinese coins called "cash" were perfect for this, as they had holes in the middle. Coin-swords were popular in south China, where they were hung in the home to ward off evil spirits.

WHITE WEDDING

Britain's Queen Victoria was the first person to popularize wearing a white wedding dress, when she wore one for her 1840 marriage to Prince Albert. Before that, brides wore colorful dresses that could be worn again following their wedding. White dresses were seen as a symbol of wealth, as it meant the family could afford to have it cleaned.

SUSPICIOUS HAIRSTYLES

Two men were stopped at Chennai International Airport in India because police officers were suspicious of their strange hairstyles. The duo was trying to smuggle gold and money under their wigs! The pair had glued pouches of cash and gold to the tops of their heads and covered them with ill-fitting hairpieces. Gold was also discovered in their socks. The total contraband confiscated was worth nearly $400,000.

FIRST JEANS

Levi Strauss and his business partner Jacob Davis patented the first pair of riveted blue jeans in 1873. The oldest blue jeans in Levi's archive date back to about 1879 and are kept in a fireproof safe. The vintage jeans are estimated to be worth $150,000.

REGULAR CUSTOMER

David Geyer, from Bergheim, Germany, has been eating at McDonald's every other day for 25 years, consuming more than 4,500 burgers in that time. He also has a tattoo of a burger and fries on his left leg, owns various items of McDonald's clothing (including sneakers and socks), and decorates his home with McDonald's memorabilia.

THROAT BLOAT

When mating season arrives, the animal kingdom gets downright wild, and this statement proves no less true when it comes to the throat-busting antics of male Masai ostriches. To advertise their interest in mating, their shins, necks, and beaks turn bright red, and the birds inflate their throats up to three times in size. Not only does this signal females to pay attention, but the swollen throat means males can create "boom" sounds to defend their territory and any girls they win over.

EXTRA EARS!

HEAR MEOW-T

Midas the cat was born with four fully functional ears!

She began her life as a stray in a backyard in Ankara, Turkey, before being adopted by Canis Dosemeci and her family. They named the kitten after the ancient Greek myth of King Midas, who the god Apollo cursed with donkey ears. Unlike the king's abnormality, Midas the cat's extra ears were caused by a genetic mutation that luckily has no negative impacts on her health. The condition also affects her jaw, causing her tongue to stick out slightly—somehow making her even more adorable!

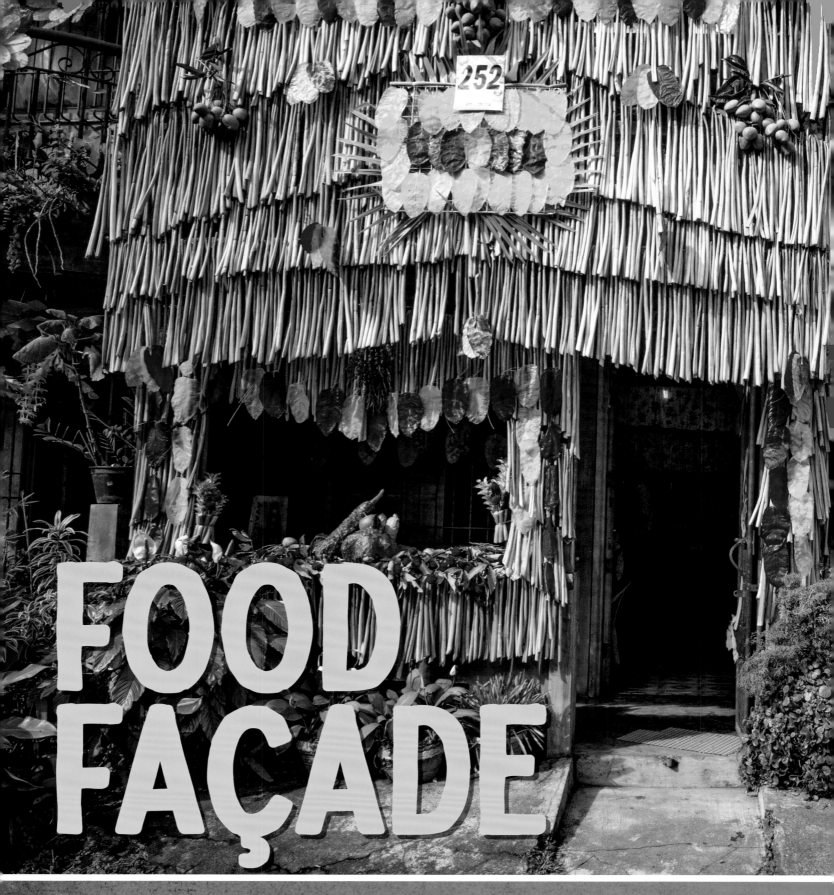

FOOD FAÇADE

The most colorful celebration in the Philippines is the Pahiyas Festival, during which locals decorate their houses with food!

The festival takes place on May 15 in Lucban, Quezon, every year. The holiday dates back to the sixteenth century when local farmers provided harvest offerings at Mount Banahaw. Today, produce is dedicated to St. Isidore the Laborer, patron saint of peasants, workers, and farmers. "Pahiyas" comes from the word "payas," meaning "to decorate." In addition to fruits and vegetables, residents also adorn their homes with products like hats, bags, sausages, and vibrant *kiping*—rice wafers shaped like leaves and dyed bright colors.

St. Isidore the Laborer, patron saint of farmers

SAILING SYMPHONY

Italian artist Livio De Marchi created a nearly 40-foot-long (12-m), 13-foot-wide (4-m) fiddle titled *Noah's Violin* that sailed through the canals of Venice carrying a performing string quartet. The musicians stood barefoot on the instrument, for better grip. Crafted from more than ten types of wood, the musically inspired vessel celebrates the city's historical connections to classical music, including famed composer Antonio Vivaldi.

LONELIEST ROAD

U.S. Route 50 in Nevada is called the "Loneliest Road in America" due to the lack of cities along the highway as it crosses uninhabited mountain passes and desert valleys. To encourage tourism, travelers can receive a survival certificate if they visit at least five checkpoints along the way.

30,000 SURGERIES

Dr. Mambet Mamakeev has been working as a surgeon in Kyrgyzstan since 1953, during which time he has treated more than 100,000 patients and performed over 30,000 surgical interventions.

YOUNG MASTER

Andrew Chen, from San Jose, California, was awarded the title of Life Master in the game of bridge just three days after his eighth birthday. Most bridge players take decades to reach that level.

CHESS SET

California jeweler Ara Ghazaryan created a tiny chess set on a board measuring just 0.31 × 0.31 inches (8 × 8 mm). The board and frame that hold it are made from gold, platinum, and Armenian apricot wood and are embedded with rubies and diamonds!

DOLL HOUSE

For Demi Moore's thirtieth birthday, Bruce Willis gave her a house just to store her collection of more than 2,000 dolls. She has since added 1,000-plus dolls to the house.

IMPRESSIVE FIND

While browsing antique books at Cambridge University's Trinity Hall for interesting stories, Head of Library Services Jenni Lecky-Thompson discovered a pressed tortoiseshell butterfly between the pages of the seventeenth-century book *Theatre of Insects*. Even more fascinating, the butterfly rested next to its accompanying printed image! Jenni speculates the butterfly could date back to the tome's 1634 publication date, and she was amazed by the beautiful color preservation of the specimen.

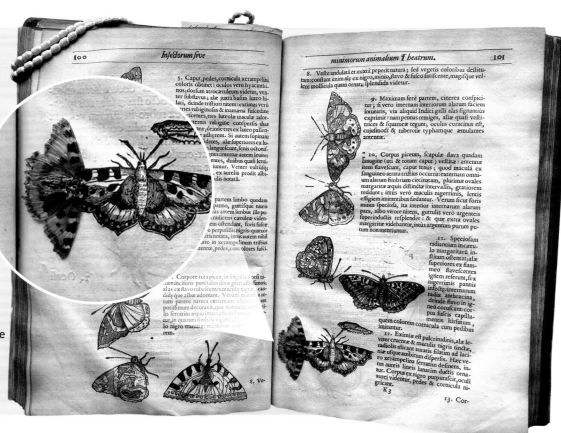

NEON BONEYARD

On an expansive plot north of Las Vegas's iconic Strip, you'll find the Neon Museum, chock full of relics that have long emblazoned the "Sin City" skyline.

Housing a collection of nearly 200 neon signs, the museum was founded in 1996 to satisfy local calls for cultural preservation. Unlike so many cities across the United States, Las Vegas has been swimming in neon artifacts for decades. So, it only made sense to create a place where they could continue to tell the city's stories even after getting replaced by updated signage. Visitors to the glittering boneyard of signs also fall in love with the museum's two resident felines, Elvis and Liberace.

BONEYARD PAR

MIGHTY MOTH

The giant wood moths of New Zealand and Australia are the heaviest moths in the world, with females weighing up to 1 ounce (30 g)—just slightly heavier than a AA battery. This might not sound like much, but in the insect world it's downright hefty! In fact, the moths are so large, they can barely fly! Spotting one of these big beauties is rare, as they only live in their flying form for about a week before dying. Prior to this, they spend about three years as larvae inside eucalyptus trees.

ENERGIZED EDDIE

Ed Gleason, of Dover Township, Pennsylvania, has ridden more than 30,000 miles (48,000 km) on his stationary bike. Even at age 76, "Energized Eddie," as he calls himself, rides at least 5 miles (8 km) every morning at a demanding 25 mph (40 kmph) pace, averaging around 1,800 miles (2,880 km) a year.

GAGA BUG

A newly discovered species of treehopper from Nicaragua has been named *Kaikaia gaga* because the bug's unique spiky horns that resemble shoulder pads reminded scientists of Lady Gaga's iconic sense of fashion.

SAME BIRTHDAY

Kate Bush, writer of the hit 1978 song "Wuthering Heights," has the same birthday— July 30—as Emily Brontë, author of the 1847 novel *Wuthering Heights*.

MINI HULK

Even though he stands just 4 feet 2 inches (1.3 m) tall after being born with dwarfism, Vince Brasco has served as a firefighter with the Greensburg, Pennsylvania, fire department for more than 13 years. He is also an accomplished bodybuilder and weightlifter nicknamed "Mini Hulk," and can bench press almost three times his body weight.

DRIVER'S VOICE

British voice-over artist Redd Pepper, who has provided trailers for movies such as *Jurassic Park*, *Space Jam*, and *Men in Black*, was discovered when he worked as a driver on the London Underground and a film executive heard one of his announcements through the train's speakers.

HARDHEADED

Australia's thorny devil has a large, false head on the back of its neck. When threatened, it hides its real head between its front legs, leaving the knob-like fake head in an upright position to confuse any would-be predators. The lizard's spikes further deter potential attackers, but extraordinary survival adaptations don't stop there. To thrive in the arid environment, tiny grooves on its skin enable the thorny devil to soak up the tiniest bits of water through capillary action, which draws the liquid right up to its mouth.

It may not look like much to you, but the rosy wolf snail has caused the extinction of more than 90 percent of Tahiti's native tree snail species.

SENSING A PATTERN

To unlock the mysteries of mass extinction in the South Pacific, scientists from the University of Michigan attached pencil eraser-sized sensors onto snail shells.

Since 1974, native tree snail species have been pushed to extinction by an invasive predator: the rosy wolf snail, which was introduced by humans hoping to eradicate a separate invasive species. Of the 61 native species of tree snail that once slithered across Tahiti, only five remain, and the sensors soon indicated how they've managed to survive. These enduring species of snails have light-colored shells and like to hang out on sunny forest floors, where the darker-shelled rosy wolf snails dare not venture. The sensors showed that their light-colored shells stopped them from overheating, while the dark shells of the rosy wolf snail make it too hot for them to last long in direct sunlight.

The native snails were too small for even the smallest sensors, so researchers opted to place the devices on the snails' favorite leaves instead.

From its humble roots in 1948 as a single burger joint, the brand known as McDonald's has exploded into a transnational corporation.

Boasting more than 36,000 locations worldwide, it has a presence in more than 100 nations and territories. But while many of the franchises have notable similarities, others stand out as both mystifying and unique. Here's what you need to know about the strangest McDonald's locations in the world.

ANGLED EATERY

Giorgi Khmaladze designed a futuristic McDonald's in Batumi, Georgia. The geometric structure features a shell of angled glass, dwarfing the brand's famous logo. The sci-fi minimalism of the structure has attracted plenty of attention and helped win the eatery Arch Daily's Best Commercial Building award in 2014.

McBARGE

The world's creepiest McDonald's is rusting in the waters off British Columbia, Canada. The dilapidated structure once represented a floating flagship, featuring a conveyor belt serving orders and a tugboat collecting water-bound rubbish. No expense was spared for its Expo 86 unveiling. But abandonment has transformed it into a nightmarish heap of decay.

FLYING SAUCER

What's the first thing you think of when you hear "Roswell"? If you're like most Americans, it's UFOs. So, it's no surprise that this famous New Mexico city boasts an out-of-this-world McDonald's. Built in the 1990s, it glows red and yellow at night and has a stellar spaceship appearance.

AIRPLANE FOOD

Taupo, New Zealand, houses an eclectic McDonald's inside a decommissioned Douglas DC-3 airplane. Opened in 2013, the franchise has become a local landmark. Guests order at a building near the plane, and roughly 20 diners can fit inside the DC-3 at a time. Visitors also enjoy scoping out the original cockpit.

TRADITIONAL TAKEOUT

This McDonald's in Fuzhou, China, symbolizes the perfect fusion between traditional architecture, cultural embellishments, and modern convenience. The structure features carved wood paneling, elaborate windows, and red paper lanterns and has become a favorite on social media and the bucket lists of architecture-crazed fast foodies.

FANCY FAST FOOD

The McDonald's Imperial in Porto, Portugal, has earned a reputation as the "World's Most Beautiful McDonald's." From its stained-glass windows to its crystal chandeliers, there's no end to the posh at this location, and visitors also claim the pastries are to die for.

McSKI

In Sweden, you'll find the McSki, a McDonald's complete with a takeout window you can ski up to. Located in Lindvallen, a ski resort town located 200 miles (322 km) north of Stockholm, it's quaint like a ski lodge and filled with the yummy goodness you expect from the golden arches.

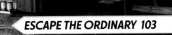

THIS IS THE WAY

ANIMAL HOUSE

Maryam al-Balushi of Muscat, Oman, shares her home with 492 furry friends, including 480 cats and 12 dogs! As you can imagine, every day is an animal party at her house, but there's nothing to celebrate when it comes to living expenses. For veterinarian care, pet food, and cleaning supplies, she spends nearly $8,000 per month. Fortunately, donations from kindhearted folks have helped her along the way. How did she get so many pets? They came to her as surrenders from local shelters and expatriates leaving the country.

Russian Star Wars fan Ayaal Fedorov created a life-size replica of helmeted bounty hunter Din Djarin's ship, the *Razor Crest*.

The Star Wars community has long cultivated a reputation for incredible feats of fandom, and this proves no less true when it comes to the spin-off series *The Mandalorian*. The DIY replica stands 13 feet (4 m) tall, 33 feet (10 m) wide, and a whopping 46 feet (14 m) long, a fitting homage to everyone's favorite space-inspired television saga. Ayaal even recreated the ship's cockpit, complete with Grogu's favorite toy—a silver knob from one of levers.

SQUAD GOALS

Few troupes have aged as gracefully as the Japan Pom Pom cheerleading squad, whose members boast an average age of 72! Fumie Takino, an energetic 90-year-old, started the group more than 26 years ago and has watched it grow from its five original members to 17 "pom pom" girls. The group meets once a week to practice and performs in competitions, breaking all stereotypes and expectations of what senior citizens are capable of. Anyone wanting to join the squad must be 55 or older and pass an audition.

CHAPEL OF BONES

Located in Évora, Portugal, is one of its most ghoulish (yet strangely beautiful) destinations in the world: the Capela dos Ossos, or Chapel of Bones.

Part of the larger Royal Church of St. Francis, the Chapel of Bones is far more than a haphazard assemblage of the dead. Instead, it represents one of the strangest interior design undertakings in history. In the sixteenth century, the monks of the church became obsessed with arranging the bones into elaborate designs. Approximately 5,000 bodies make up the morbid interior. The overarching vision behind the strange necropolis is summarized in the inscription over the door: "We bones that are here, await yours."

"We bones that are here, await yours."

KEEPING TRACT

When it comes to massive collections, objects typically number in the hundreds or thousands. But Phil Warren's collection of "just" 83 items is still impressive when you realize he collects tractors! The Devon, England, man purchased his first tractor in 1989 and amassed an incredible collection over the next three decades. All of them are vintage Ford models built between 1965 and 1976. In 2021, Phil sold much of his collection in the hopes of bringing enjoyment to a new generation of collectors.

INVISIBLE SCULPTURE

An empty space titled "I Am" by Italian artist Salvatore Garau sold for over $18,000 in 2021 as an invisible sculpture! Garau, who gave the buyer a certificate of authenticity to prove that the artwork was real, described his sculpture as "made of air and spirit."

CAT ALLERGY

Brie Larson performed daring stunts in the *Captain Marvel* movie, including a judo throw on a moving train, but could not cope with being in the same room as a cat. Larson is highly allergic to felines, so her scenes with Carol Danvers's pet cat Goose were filmed either with a puppet or by using computer-generated effects.

EXPENSIVE COPY

An unknown seventeenth-century Italian artist's copy by of Leonardo da Vinci's iconic early sixteenth-century painting *Mona Lisa* sold at auction in Paris, France, in 2021 for $3.4 million.

FLAG CHANGE

The Canadian flag on top of the Peace Tower in Ottawa, Ontario, is changed every weekday. To replace it, the flag master must climb 110 feet (33 m) of stairs and ladders, and throughout the half-hour changeover, the flag must never be allowed to touch the ground. Canadian citizens can apply to receive one of the old flags for free, but the current waiting list is around 99 years.

COFFEE ROUTINE

Nineteenth-century Danish philosopher Søren Kierkegaard had 50 sets of cups and saucers for coffee. Each day his secretary would be required to decide which set to use and to explain to him the reasons behind her decision.

DOUBLE CELEBRATION

On May 2, 2021, at Marshfield Medical Center in Eau Claire, Wisconsin, siblings Katie Ross and Jacob Luttropp welcomed new babies within less than two hours of each other. Shortly after Katie and her husband Matt had a baby boy named Finley, Jacob and his wife Caitlin had a daughter, Maeve. Both babies were delivered by the same midwife.

CORAL CROCHET

Textile artist Gioni Gessele of Klamath Falls, Oregon, spent 14 months crocheting this one-of-a-kind coral reef!

The vibrant display measures 3 feet (0.9 m) tall, 6 feet (1.8 m) long, and 3 feet (0.9 m) wide when fully assembled. Hidden in the reef are two seahorses, a clownfish, and a yellow-and-white sea snake all made from yarn. Besides the intricacy of each creature, one of its most remarkable features is the variety of colors used and how they glow under a black light! Gioni crafted this marine masterpiece to bring awareness to climate change and warming ocean waters, which cause coral reefs to lose their color and die.

IT GLOWS!

STICK TRICK

Spiders in the *Poltys* genus take camouflage to the next level with their incredible ability to hide in plain sight as sticks, leaves, and even tree stumps! These amazing arachnids spend their nights spinning traditional webs, hoping to capture a moth or two in the process. They rest during the day, relying on their confusing appearances to avoid being devoured by birds and other predators.

WOOD PREPPERS

Acorn woodpeckers will spend hours meticulously tapping thousands of small, uniform holes into tree trunks (or even telephone poles and wooden house siding), creating individual storage units for the acorns they collect. These unmistakable trees are known as "granaries," named after the aboveground storehouses farmers use to keep grain away from pests. Believe it or not, multiple generations of acorn woodpeckers will use the same granary tree for years!

OPEN WIDE

In 1992, two girls in Ontario stumbled upon a fascinating natural discovery: a toad with eyes on the roof of its mouth!

According to Scott Gardner, the newspaper photographer who captured the oddity on film, the toad appeared to gain greater awareness of its surroundings when it opened its mouth, suggesting the eyes were perfectly functional. The anomaly was caused by a genetic phenomenon called a "macromutation," which is a mutation that makes a significant impact on an organism. What exactly caused the macromutation, however, remains a mystery.

CLOSE ENCOUNTER

While kayaking and whale watching off the coast of Avila Beach, California, Julie McSorley and Liz Cottriel almost ended up in the mouth of a huge humpback whale that surfaced beneath their boat, capsizing it and lifting them above the water. Despite fearing that they might be swallowed alive, the duo emerged unharmed.

STOWAWAY CAT

Panda, a tuxedo cat owned by Christina and Josh Clevenger, wandered away from its home in Thurston County, Washington, hitched a ride in a shipping container, and ended up at a Home Depot store 10 days later—about 2,500 miles (4,000 km) away in Kenai, Alaska!

BIN RACE

Street cleaners in Zagreb, Croatia, have custom-made tricycles with trash cans chained onto the front, and every year they race these around the city streets at alarming speeds, cornering wildly on just two wheels.

CANNED STONES

The Choshi Electric Railway in Japan's Chiba Prefecture sells cans of stones from beneath its tracks. The stones are washed and waxed before being packaged. They sell for about $15 a can and are marketed as excellent paperweights and collectible items for train enthusiasts. The railway claims you can hear a train if you hold one of the stones to your ear!

CREEPY DISH

Invented in the early 2000s by a restaurateur in Taiwan, Yin Yang fish is a controversial dish where the body of the fish is cooked but the head is preserved raw so that the fish moves its mouth and eyes while it is being eaten. The head is wrapped in ice cubes and the rest fried so quickly before being served that, while not actually alive, it still produces uncontrolled nerve spasms on the plate.

DUMMY DOWNHILL

The Mount Ashland ski resort in Oregon holds an annual event called the Dummy Downhill. Each handmade dummy must weigh less than 125 pounds (57 kg) and be mounted on either a pair of skis or a snowboard. The themed dummies are pushed down a hill by their creators and are judged on artistic creativity, their time spent in the air as they tackle a jump, and the general quality of their run.

ROTATING HOUSE

A house near Verona, Italy, rotates on a large turntable so that it can follow the sun across the sky and absorb as much sunlight as possible during the day. The rotation of the L-shaped Villa Girasole, which means "Sunflower House" in Italian, is controlled by its occupants.

ORANGE GLOW

The world's first 3D-printed lamp made from orange peels has made its debut, featuring a sleek, repurposed design.

Known as the Ohmie Lamp, it's the brainchild of Krill Design and is both functional and aesthetically pleasing. Its clean lines and minimal sophistication provide a stunning reminder of how food waste can be utilized. As an added bonus, it smells like orange cookies when illuminated!

STYLE & SUBSTANCE

One of the trendiest pieces of Victorian jewelry also proved to be highly functional: the chatelaine, an extravagant equivalent of a Swiss Army knife.

These elaborate silver accessories contained a variety of tools customized to the wearer's interests. For example, a nurse's chatelaine might have safety pins and a thermometer. And a chatelaine for a seamstress might include a thimble, a needle case, and a tape measure. Over time, these items verged away from functionality toward aesthetics, leading to even more impressive designs.

Ripley's Exhibit
Cat. No. 172846

SKULL BORING TOOL

An 1800s medical tool used to bore a hole into the skull in order to relieve pressure, a process called *trepanation*. One of the oldest medical procedures known to man, trepanation has been performed since 6500 BC, based on skulls found in a burial site in France in the 1680s.

THIS SKULL FROM PERU SHOWS EVIDENCE OF TREPANATION!

Ripley's Exhibit
Cat. No. 23580

TRANSATLANTIC CABLE

A 4-inch (10-cm) piece of the first transatlantic cable. This technology shortened the length of time to communicate between North America and Europe from 10 days to just hours. The first message was sent on August 16, 1858. The excess cable from this venture was purchased by Tiffany & Company of New York, snipped into short pieces, and sold as souvenirs.

Ripley's Exhibit
Cat. No. 173038

EDISON LAMP

Commemorative lamp from the 1929 "Light's Golden Jubilee" event held in honor of Thomas Edison's transformative invention, the incandescent lightbulb. U.S. President Hoover, businessman Henry Ford, scientist Marie Curie, aviation pioneer Orville Wright, and Edison himself are just some of the big names who attended the party, which included a dramatic reenactment of when Edison turned the first incandescent lamp on in 1879.

The
MIRACLE
of
1879
Thos. A. Edison's
FIRST LAMP

LIGHT'S GOLDEN JUBILEE

HAPPY NUDE YEAR!

For the past 500 years, residents of Okayama, Japan, have celebrated New Year's by assembling more than 10,000 loincloth-clad men who try their luck at catching talismans thrown into the crowd.

During the event, the sea of semi-nude men takes the mosh pit concept to the next level as they lunge, twist, and wrestle to grab hold of two little sticks—symbols of good fortune. Besides auspicious tidings, participating in the festival comes with the possibility of a fruitful harvest. Known locally as the Saidaiji Eyo Festival, it remains the most famous of the Hadaka Matsuri (Naked Men Festivals) in Japan.

COLOSSAL CASTLE

Wilfred Stijger of the Netherlands created a 69-foot-tall (21.16-m) sandcastle in Blokhus, Denmark. It required a team of 30 individuals to construct and contained a staggering 4,680 tons of sand. Besides its massive size, the structure boasted imagery related to current events. Its elaborate construction won the admiration of other record-breaking sandcastle builders who have likened it to a classical or medieval architectural masterpiece.

STONE GIANT

Towering 35 feet (10.67 meters) above the ground, the *Apennine Colossus* is a massive sculpture created by the sixteenth-century artist known as Giambologna. Located at the Villa Demidoff in Tuscany, Italy, the masterpiece depicts a personification of the country's Apennine Mountains. The statue's massive scale leads many to believe Giambologna was inspired by the titan Atlas of Greek mythology. But perhaps the most fascinating parts of the creation are the many water cascades and cave-like rooms hidden within the statue.

EARLY BIRD

Eighty-three-year-old Angelo Boletti, from Castiraga Vidardo, Italy, was fined $200 because his rooster named Carlino crowed too early in the morning. The bird started crowing at 4:30 a.m. and repeatedly woke Boletti's neighbors.

BOTH HANDS

Sixteen-year-old Aadi Swaroopa, of Mangalore, India, can write 45 words in one minute, using both hands at the same time—and in different languages. Ambidextrous Aadi, who could reportedly write 30 pages when she was only 30 months old, can write simultaneously in English and Kannada, a southern Indian language.

POPULAR PUDDLE

A huge, 26-year-old puddle on a street in the Russian city of Yuzhno-Sakhalinsk has its own Instagram page and more than 10,000 followers. It started out as a small pothole, but left unrepaired by the local council, it has grown in size to the point where it covers most of the street.

SINISTER SNAKE

Kukri snakes from Asia use their sharp, curved fangs to slice into their victims, such as frogs and venomous toads, and then eat them alive from the inside. Sometimes they disembowel their prey by opening the frog's belly and inserting their head into the frog's abdomen. By tearing out the organs and swallowing them one by one, the snake keeps its hapless prey alive for a few traumatic hours.

SWEARING PARROTS

Five African gray parrots at Lincolnshire Wildlife Park in England were temporarily removed from public view in September 2020 after they began swearing at visitors.

POOP COFFEE

Jacu bird coffee is made from coffee cherries eaten, digested, and excreted by jacu birds in southeast Brazil. The bird poop coffee costs around $1,000 for 2.2 pounds (1 kg) because of its exclusivity.

MOSQUITO TORNADO

In the summer of 2021, villages in Kamchatka, Russia, experienced mosquito tornadoes, where billions of insects formed massive swirls in the sky. The tornadoes, which were visible from miles away, were caused by the mosquitoes' mating ritual when thousands of males swarm around a female.

JOINT SOVEREIGNTY

Each year, Pheasant Island is part of Spain from February 1 to July 31 and part of France for the other six months. The 656-foot-long (200-m), 131-foot-wide (40-m), uninhabited island on the Bidasoa River that separates France and Spain was placed under the joint sovereignty of the two countries by the 1659 Treaty of the Pyrenees.

FACIAL AMNESIA

Lena Pepel, a young woman from Russia, has the rare condition prosopagnosia, which means that she cannot recognize faces—not even her own looking back at her in the mirror! In order to identify people, she has to memorize their voices.

PENNY DROP

Four months after Andreas Flaten quit his job at an auto repair shop in Peachtree City, Georgia, his former employer delivered his final payment of $915 in the form of 91,500 grease-covered pennies dumped on his driveway.

DOUBLE WIN

Orlene Peterson, of Coeur d'Alene, Idaho, won $200,000 from a scratch-off lottery ticket she bought on January 29, 2021, and then won a further $300,000 from another ticket she bought the next day. The double win beat odds of 1 in 282.5 million.

ORANGE POWER

The Spanish city of Seville converts its leftover oranges into electricity. The methane from the fermented fruits is captured and then used to power a generator. The city has around 48,000 orange trees, which deposit 12,500,000 pounds (5,700,000 kg) of fruit on the streets in winter—enough to power 73,000 homes.

DRY SPOT

The 2,000-foot-high (609-m) Friis Hills in Antarctica have seen little to no rainfall for 14 million years. Dry and barren, the area receives an average of only 0.24 inches (6 mm) of water per year in the form of tiny amounts of snow that drift in from surrounding valleys.

ANT-EGG SOUP

A traditional dish enjoyed in Thailand and Laos, ant-egg soup features an unlikely ingredient: the eggs of red weaver ants.

The eggs develop in silk nests woven by the ants, making them easy to see. But that doesn't mean they're easy to get; red weaver ants never stray far from these nests, and if you try to cut the branch of a tree to get to them, you'll end up covered in the six-legged biting critters. Once harvested, the ivory-white eggs, which look like tiny white beans and explode in the mouth like caviar, mark the highlight of the spicy soup, bobbing atop a bed of vegetables and pieces of fish.

LIVING DEAD

Over the past few centuries, humans have witnessed (and contributed to) the extinction of various species, from the dodo bird to the Tasmanian tiger.

Against all odds, some animals previously thought to be gone forever have reappeared, giving researchers cause for celebration. These creatures are known as "Lazarus animals" because of their apparent ability to rise from the dead. Here are seven that have returned from the brink of non-existence.

COELACANTH

Overcoming 66 million years of extinction isn't easy, but that's what the coelacanth has done. Referred to as a "living fossil," this incredible fish was rediscovered in 1938 off the South African coast. It swims up to 2,300 feet (700 m) beneath the ocean's surface and can measure more than 6 feet (1.8 m) long, weigh nearly 200 pounds (90.7 kg), and live for 60 years.

SINGING DOG

An ancient species related to the Australian dingo, the New Zealand singing dog went five decades with no sightings. But in remote New Guinea, scientists stumbled across a new population in 2016. Known for their high-pitched singing, they often join together in choruses and will hopefully continue singing into the future.

CHINESE CRESTED TERNS

In the late twentieth century, Chinese crested terns were added to the extinction list, where they stayed until the year 2000. That's when researchers exploring the Mazu Islands off the coast of Fujian Province discovered eight of the presumed-dead birds. Since then, restoration efforts have grown the population to over 100.

TREE LOBSTERS

Lord Howe Island stick insects, a.k.a. tree lobsters, resemble miniature land-bound crustaceans, and were presumed extinct in 1920 after predatory rats were inadvertently introduced to the island. But in 2001, a pair of the Australian bugs turned up alive and well! Captured and bred, researchers hope their efforts will lead to the successful repopulation of the species.

OMURA'S WHALE

A few dead specimens found in 2003 were all researchers had to go off of when officially describing the Omura's whale. Scientists didn't expect to learn much about the presumed-extinct species until a pod showed up off the coast of Madagascar in 2013, representing the first confirmed sightings of the marine mammal alive.

PYGMY TARSIERS

Nocturnal primates found in the jungles of Indonesia, pygmy tarsiers were declared extinct in the early twentieth century. So, researchers couldn't believe their eyes after these amber-eyed critters reappeared in the early 2000s! Scientists have placed tracking collars on a handful of the creatures to gain valuable information that could help preserve the species.

ARAKAN FOREST TURTLE

Native to Myanmar, the Arakan forest turtle topped the extinction list in 1908. But more than 80 years later, in 1994, researchers rediscovered it in an unlikely place: Asian food markets. Touted as having medicinal properties, the turtle faces many challenges in the future, from loss of habitat to being hunted for food.

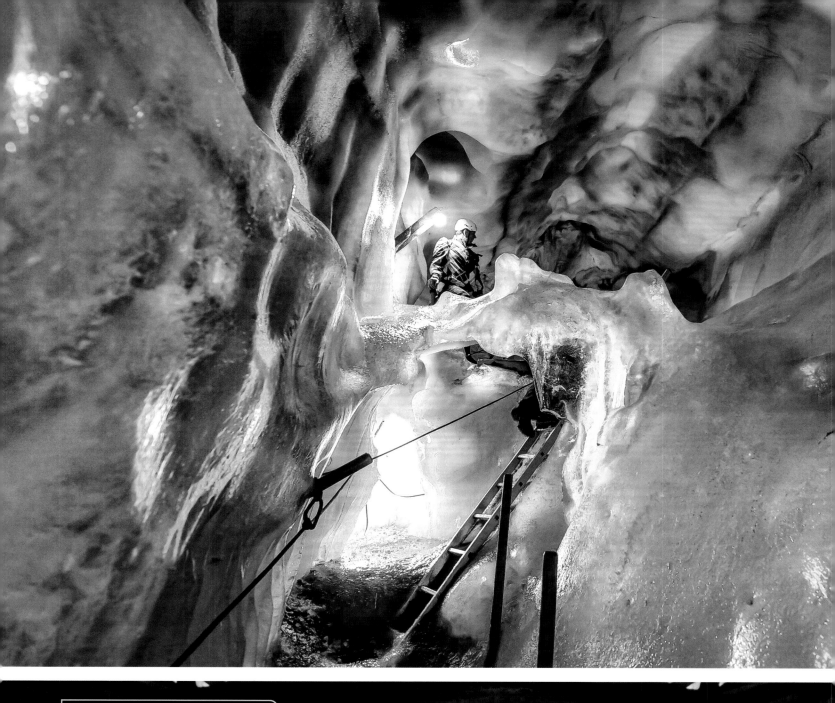

INSIDE VOICES

Believe it or not, by using a technique called "forcing," farmers can get rhubarb to grow so fast that you can actually hear it! "Forcing" involves raising the vegetable in dark sheds, which results in a sweeter and more tender crop than rhubarb grown outside. At times, a popping and crackling can be heard inside the candle-lit sheds—the sound of rhubarb growing several inches in a day!

FROZEN FUN

Inside Hintertux Glacier in Austria, you'll find Nature's Ice Palace (Natur Eis Palast), a frozen cave more than 10,000 feet (3,048 m) above sea level.

The location was discovered relatively recently in 2007 by Austrian ski guide Roman Erler, who now offers tours at Nature's Ice Palace. Visitors young and old can take a boat tour, hike, and even paddle a kayak through the Palace's chilly tunnels. Believe it or not, one of the most popular activities is swimming! Swimmers with a fondness for ice-induced pain test their skills in 20-meter and 75-meter-long events, all while staving off the real possibility of hypothermia.

95 MARATHONS

Alyssa Clark of Panama City, Florida, ran a full marathon in Italy every day for 95 days straight, running 2,489 miles (4,006 km) between March 31 and July 3, 2020.

TOAST CASTLE

Matt Close, an engineer from Lancashire, England, built a lifelike model of Lancaster Castle entirely out of toast! It took him five hours and he used two loaves of bread.

EIGHT-DAY STREAM

A 2020 livestream by Twitch video game streamer Louis Sammartino of New Jersey went on for 195 hours 36 minutes and 17 seconds—that's more than eight days. He had pledged to extend his stream for two minutes for every new subscription he received to his channel.

Using drumsticks, six-year-old Devaagyh Dixit, from Lucknow, India, can perform 5,570 drum beats in only three minutes. He has been drumming since he was just two.

AIRPLANE WRECKAGE

While walking their dog on Cleethorpes Beach in Lincolnshire, England, in 2020, couple Debi Hartley and Graham Holden discovered the wreckage of a World War II fighter plane. The Royal Air Force plane had crash-landed after taking off from a nearby airfield in 1944, and even after 76 years, the ammunition on board was still live, forcing a bomb disposal team to conduct a controlled explosion.

STOMACH OPENING

After being accidentally shot with a musket at close range in 1822, Canadian fur trapper Alexis St. Martin lived with a hole in his stomach for 58 years. U.S. Army surgeon William Beaumont used St. Martin as a guinea pig for around 200 experiments to study the human digestive system. Beaumont would dangle food on a string into the hole in St. Martin's stomach and later pull it out to observe to what extent it had been digested.

VOLCANO CLIMBER

In addition to climbing the tallest mountain on all seven continents, Australian adventurer Daniel Bull has climbed the highest volcano on each continent. He has also kayaked on a lake 18,723 feet (5,708 m) above sea level on the Ojos del Salado volcano in Chile after using an axe to smash through the ice on the water's surface.

TORTOISE ON WHEELS

Helmuth, a 220-pound (100-kg) African spurred tortoise at a zoo in North Rhine-Westphalia, Germany, was fitted with a roller board to overcome joint pain in his front legs and help him move around more easily.

POOL RESCUE

When Chucky, a toy Pomeranian, fell into the backyard pool of Byron and Melissa Thanarayen's home in Boksburg, South Africa, and immediately began to struggle in the water, the little pup was rescued by the couple's other dog, Jessie, a Staffordshire bull terrier. After several unsuccessful attempts spanning over half an hour, Jessie was finally able to lift the exhausted Chucky out of the water with her mouth.

NUMBER TENS

There is an exact replica of the front of the British Prime Minister's London residence, 10 Downing Street, a ten-minute walk away at 10 Adam Street. The fake Downing Street is often used for tourist photos.

PORCELAIN PLATES

Every inch of the interior and exterior walls of Nguyen Van Truong's home in Kieu Son, Vietnam, is decorated with 10,000 porcelain bowls, plates, and urns. Even his garden fence and gate are covered in the porcelain dishes that he has been collecting for over 30 years.

SKY MANSION

A replica of the White House stands atop the 32-floor Kingfisher Tower in Bangalore. The luxury mansion in the sky was built on the orders of Indian businessman Vijay Mallya.

SAME NAME

When actor Dennis Quaid saw a story on TV about a six-year-old black cat named Dennis Quaid living at an animal shelter in Lynchburg, Virginia, he adopted the cat for his office in Los Angeles.

PUPPY LOVE

When Nashville, Tennessee, businessman Bill Dorris died in 2020 at age 84, he left $5 million in his will to Lulu, his border collie dog.

TASTE BUDS

Some large species of catfish have 180,000 taste buds located all over their body. By contrast, humans have about 10,000 taste buds.

FAN FEED

CLIP ART

Midhun RR of India crafts detailed works of art out of human hair! The artist began working with the unusual material in 2017 after he was left with an abundance of people's hair following a project in which he built mud walls reinforced with natural fibers, including salon clippings. To create his pieces, Midhun must work in a room alone while wearing a mask, so he doesn't send the shavings flying with his breath. To date, he's crafted more than 25 hair artworks, including portraits of Marilyn Monroe and a hairy rendition of Leonardo da Vinci's *The Last Supper*.

SELF(LESS) PORTRAIT

Despite being a machine powered by artificial intelligence, Ai-Da—the world's first ultra-realistic robot artist—creates portraits of herself.

Ai-Da began her career working in abstract art, but the strangely lifelike AI has now moved into the realm of creating self-portraits. While looking into a mirror with her camera-eyes, Ai-Da's algorithms drive the movement of her drawing hand across the paper. The purpose behind her self-portraits is to make people question "the nature of human identity and creativity." As one of her creators, Aidan Meller, noted, "It is literally the world's first self-portrait with no self." Nevertheless, Ai-Da's work has been featured in museums and galleries around the world.

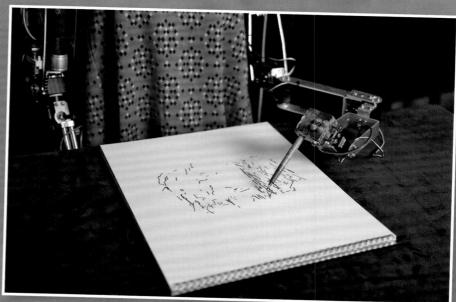

TOP BANANA

In Borneo's Tanjung Puting National Park, photographer Sergey Savvi captured the incredible moment when a hungry orangutan climbed a 49-foot-tall (15-m) tree with 14 bananas stuffed in her mouth! Fruit poking out of her mouth in every direction, the multitasking primate also held a baby in one arm. Fortunately, both mom and baby made the trip safely, enjoying a banana feast from the treetops.

SHARK ATTACK
A 19-foot-long (5.8-m) great white shark chomped on the back of Danny McDaniel's kayak while he was kayaking off Catalina Island in Camp Emerald Bay, California, leaving two huge teeth behind as evidence.

HEROIC PUPPY
When Doug Gillman of Columbus, Ohio, stopped breathing while asleep in an armchair, his life was saved by his family's eight-month-old pit bull Charley, who alerted Doug's wife Felicia by waking her up. The puppy barked and then jumped on Felicia's lap to rouse her before immediately sitting on Doug's knee and licking him. When he didn't respond, Felicia knew something was wrong and called for medical help.

SAVED BACON
A pig started a fire at a farm in West Yorkshire, England, by defecating after eating a battery-operated pedometer. The copper from the pedometer's batteries reacted with the pig poop and dry hay to spark a blaze, which firefighters managed to extinguish before any animals were hurt.

ODD COUPLE
At the Mia Foundation, an animal rescue group in Rochester, New York, a flightless pigeon befriended a puppy who can't walk. The center's founder, Sue Rogers, took in Herman the pigeon after seeing him struggling to move around in a car dealership parking lot, and he soon made friends with tiny chihuahua puppy Lundy, who has problems with his hind legs. The pair cuddle up together on their favorite fluffy blanket.

HIVE OF ACTIVITY
When Herb Herbert called in experts to deal with the bee problem he had been experiencing in his El Cajon, California, backyard for more than two years, they discovered a 30-inch-long (75-cm) beehive weighing 70 pounds (32 kg) under his shed—with more than 100,000 bees living there.

EARN YOUR STRIPES

Wildlife photographer Anja Denker captured images of a zebra with a black-splotch-patterned coat in Namibia's Etosha National Park. Researchers believe the animal has a pigmentation disorder, expressed by a predominance of dark stripes. The creature's survival is impressive, as other zebras with similar coloring have been known to be easier targets for predators and typically don't last long in the wild.

GAS CONTROL

Manatees use their flatulence to determine how they swim. They regulate the distribution of their internal gases, choosing to hold in gas to be more buoyant and reach the surface or release gas when they want to dive. An adult manatee eats up to 150 pounds (68 kg) of vegetation every day, so a lot of methane builds up inside its body.

DEADLY PASSENGER

K. A. Ranjith rode his motorbike for nearly 7 miles (11.2 km) to Kandanad, India, before realizing that for the entire journey a venomous snake—a common krait—had been coiled up inside the helmet he was wearing. It was only when Ranjith removed his helmet that he saw the snake, which had been crushed to death over the course of the ride.

TURTLE POWER

The *Stupendemys geographicus* turtle, which lived in South America 13 million years ago before the Amazon and Orinoco Rivers were formed, was around 13 feet (4 m) long and weighed 1.25 tons, making it the size of a car.

UNIQUE PATTERN

Every individual blue poison dart frog has a unique pattern of black spots on its back and sides—like a fingerprint—that can be used to tell them apart.

MATING CALL

After a male peacock named Snowbank escaped from Franklin Park Zoo in Boston, Massachusetts, he was recaptured with the help of an electronic mating call. A quick-thinking police officer searched for a peacock mating call on his cell phone, and when he played it, the bird was lured into a secure area until zoo officials arrived.

HURRICANE ORDEAL

Three cows swept out to sea from Cedar Island, North Carolina, by the 8-foot-high (2.4-m) waves of Hurricane Dorian in 2019 were found alive and well two months later on a remote island on the Outer Banks. The cows are believed to have swum around 5 miles (8 km) to safety.

SURPRISE SUSPECT

Police officers investigating damage to an ATM at a bank kiosk in Delhi, India, reviewed security footage and saw that the culprit breaking into the cash machine was not a human but a monkey! The video showed the monkey removing the ATM's front panel, then climbing inside to inspect it before eventually running off empty-handed.

MUSICAL MOTH

The male mandolin moth of Eastern Europe is so named because its hind wings are concave like a mandolin—and when it is time to mate, the male serenades the female by scratching a knotted vein on his wing with his hind leg to produce a tune.

DOUBLE DRUMSTICKS

Interested in learning more about the tiny limbs dangling from the fluffy chick's rear, Rebecca researched the topic online. She discovered that the strange-looking chick had a rare congenital condition known as polymelia (literally "many limbs"). Typically, polymelia results in malformed or underdeveloped extra limbs. But in the case of Rebecca's petite chicken, it added two fully formed, though non-functioning, legs.

WINE AND DINE

Wine lovers will fall head over heels for the Dürkheimer Riesenfaß, located in Bad Dürkheim, Germany.

Crafted from the largest wine barrel in the world, it boasts a diameter of 44 feet (13.5 m) and a capacity of 449,092 gallons (1.7 million liters). But the gigantic structure holds restaurant goers rather than wine. The colossal barrel was constructed in 1934 by the vineyard owner and master cooper Fritz Keller.

HOMESICK RETRIEVER

After going missing from Drew Feeback's home in Olathe, Kansas, four-year-old golden retriever Cleo turned up a week later at the front door of the family's former home in Lawson, Missouri—more than 50 miles (80.5 km) away! The family had moved two years earlier, and Cleo had to cross busy roads and a river to reach her old home.

LATEX FEET

More than 1,600 pairs of latex ears and feet were used in the movie *The Lord of the Rings: The Fellowship of the Ring*, each cooked in a special oven that ran 24 hours a day, seven days a week. The feet could not be removed at the end of a day's filming without damaging them, so each pair could only be used once.

SLEEP VIDEO

On February 9, 2020, Chinese actor and social media user Yuansan livestreamed himself sleeping for five hours, primarily to find out whether he snores—but when he woke up he discovered that he had attracted 800,000 new followers for his channel. When he repeated the exercise, it brought in 18 million views and his channel went viral.

BUN RUN

The Cheung Chau Bun Festival in Hong Kong is one of the liveliest and most exhilarating in Asia, showcasing bamboo mountains taller than buildings and decked out in handmade buns.

The towers are part of a competition in which participants race to the top, grabbing as many buns as they can along the way. Besides incredible pillars of lucky bun treats, you'll also see many colorful food offerings as well as vendors peddling vibrant decorations and trinkets. Children hold a unique role in the celebrations, dressed as Chinese mythological deities and held aloft on stands above the crowds. The festival also features parades with lion dances, marching bands, and martial arts demonstrations accompanied by percussive cymbals and drums.

GOING GREEN

Ali Spagnola of Los Angeles, California, transformed her car into a giant Chia Pet by covering it with a thick carpet of living plants!

Having previously covered her car in blue artificial turf, Ali decided to take things to the next level. She started with science experiments to determine the best way to grow a living mural on a vehicle, relying on suggestions from moss art experts. After deciding on well-hydrated chia seed paste, she spent two hours hand painting her hatchback's fake grass surface with the pasty seed mixture. Six days of careful watering yielded an automobile covered in a 2-inch-thick (5-cm) layer of lush, living plants! Ali then took to the streets of LA, putting a smile on plenty of faces along the way.

IT'S ALIVE!

MUD ART

For his piece titled *Challenging Mud*, avant-garde Japanese artist Kazuo Shiraga stripped down to a pair of shorts and writhed around in a pool of wet mud, leaving a series of impressions on the mud with his cut and bruised body. For another piece, he attached ropes to the ceiling, dipped his feet in paint, and swung back and forth, painting on a canvas floor.

METAL PAWS

Dymka, a four-year-old cat from Russia, was given four titanium, 3D-printed prosthetic paws after her own were badly damaged by frostbite. The metal paws were created by veterinarian Sergei Gorshkov and researchers from Tomsk Polytechnic University. Thanks to the surgery, Dymka can now walk, run, play, and climb stairs.

FLAWED FORECAST

When the 2013 movie *The Great Gatsby* was being filmed in Australia's Blue Mountains, the crew purchased 22,000 gallons (83,000 liters) of water on a beautiful spring day to create the synthetic rain required for an upcoming scene because a private meteorologist had assured them that the forecast was for dry weather. Instead, it rained naturally for the next three days.

SNAKE CATCHER

After snake catcher Stewart Gatt was called out to relocate a female tiger snake from a resident's yard in Ardeer, Victoria, Australia, the snake gave birth in his car—and one of its babies had two heads.

LONG PROCESS

German composer Johannes Brahms was such a perfectionist that his Symphony No. 1 took 21 years from when he started writing it to its first performance in 1876.

MERCY MISSION

Determined 15-year-old Jyoti Kumari pedaled 750 miles (1,200 km) by bicycle while carrying her injured father, Mohan Paswan, as a passenger. With her father sitting on the rear carrier, she completed the ride from his workplace in Gurugram, India, to their home in Darbhanga in less than two weeks.

CUNNING CAMOUFLAGE

Feeding on frogs and lizards, the long-nosed vine snake of Southeast Asia is camouflaged to look like a green vine growing up through the branches of trees. The snake weighs so little that it can successfully move from one branch to another with half of its body hanging in mid-air.

FAST READER

John F. Kennedy taught himself to read 1,200 words per minute—six times the speed of the average person. He could also speak very fast, and in a 1961 speech he was timed at an incredible 327 words per minute.

FIERCE FACIAL HAIR

The male Emei mustache toad of China grows spines on its upper lip, giving it the appearance of spiky facial hair! Each frog grows between 10 and 16 spines. According to researchers, the points are about as sharp as pencil lead, and the amphibians use them like defensive spikes when bothered by a predator or a competing male.

Female Emei mustache toad sans mustache.

BARKOUR

Parkour has gone to the dogs (literally!) in the form of barkour, and one of the masters of the art is a canine named Ninja.

How did Ninja get involved in barkour in the first place? Through his owner Dominik "Dodo" Arend, a parkour instructor and dog trainer. Dodo trained the dynamic pooch, relying on the same philosophy he uses with his human students—learning to face and overcome fear. The result? Not only is Ninja capable of incredible agility tricks, he's also developed into a highly self-confident canine capable of learning anything.

Ripley's Exhibit
Cat. No. 173420

SCRAP METAL PREDATOR

A scrap metal version of the alien species from the *Predator* films. Created by a group of artists in Thailand who specialize in transforming leftover or discarded metal pieces into highly detailed pop culture recreations. This piece incorporates a multitude of colors, which allows details to stand out—such as the human skull impaled on the spear.

Ripley's Exhibit
Cat. No. 175282
BUTTONS SPIDER-MAN

Created by Brandon Trujillo, this life-size recreation of Peter Parker's alter-ego is made from thousands of buttons! Besides the unique medium, what makes this sculpture stand out is that it doesn't stand at all! Instead, it hangs from the ceiling in that iconic Spider-Man pose.

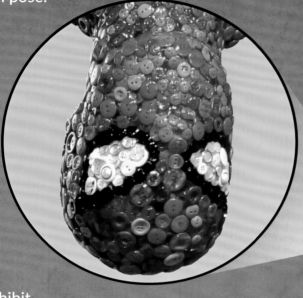

Ripley's Exhibit
Cat. No. 172846
STAR TREK: FIRST CONTACT CONSOLE

This engineering console is a set piece from the 1996 film *Star Trek: First Contact*. It sat on the bridge of the starship USS *Enterprise-E* and was manned by Starfleet officer Geordi La Forge, played by LeVar Burton. The empty center panels held monitors for changing images. Set builders added little jokes into the small details that wouldn't be caught by cameras, including a *Looney Tunes* reference!

047 | OPTICAL DATA NET SERVICE ACCESS
CAUTION: OPERATING PROTOCOL 95-7574 REQUIRES FULL REDUNDANCY FOR ALL PRIMARY DATA FEEDS. BE VEWY, VEWY QWIET, I'M HUNTING WABBITS. HEH HEH HEH!

FAST AND CURIOUS

Jonny Davies (a.k.a. "Stunter Jonny") of County Durham, Ireland, performed a handlebar wheelie while speeding the roadway at a whopping 109.2 mph (175.7 kmph)! Perhaps most impressive is Jonny's background. A maintenance technician, "Stunter Jonny" only started riding motorcycles in excess of 100 mph (161 kmph) a year prior to this death-defying stunt.

TWISTED TOENAILS

Arinda Storm Weaver, from Columbus, Ohio, has allowed her toenails to grow so that some are more than 6 inches (15 cm) long. Because her nails are so long and twisted, she has to wear open-toed sandals to keep them from breaking. Her fingernails are also very long, meaning that she cannot wear any clothes with buttons.

LOOM BAND

Crafty 10-year-old Mark Millar of Broughshane, Northern Ireland, wove a loom band bracelet that was nearly 6,292 feet (1,918 m) long—more than a mile. It took almost a year to make and four hours just to measure it.

GAMING GRANDMA

Ninety-year-old Japanese grandmother Hamako Mori has been playing video games for nearly 40 years. The "Gamer Grandma" plays her PlayStation 4 to an audience of more than 530,000 subscribers on YouTube. One of her favorite games is *Grand Theft Auto V*.

HISTORIC SPIN

An 11-year-old Brazilian boy, Gui Khury, became the first skateboarder ever to land a 1080-degree spin on a vertical ramp. Using makeshift facilities in his grandmother's back garden, he completed three full rotations on his board before making a clean landing. At age eight, he became the youngest boarder to pull off a 900-degree spin.

FOOT ARTIST

Born without arms due to a rare disorder called tetra-amelia syndrome, Colombian artist Linda Riveros paints with her feet, holding the brush precisely between the two largest toes on her right foot. She began painting with her feet when she was seven and has had a number of solo exhibitions near her home in Peekskill, New York.

LEGO HOUSE

Andy Romaniszyn spent a year creating a replica of his two-story home in Greater Manchester, England, using 3,152 LEGO bricks, faithfully replicating every room down to the smallest detail. He used the original blueprints of the house to ensure that the scale of his model was accurate and even included a miniature version of the LEGO house inside the replica.

EMPTY BAGS

Gary Key, from East Yorkshire, England, has been collecting empty potato chip packets since 2012 and has built up a collection of more than 14,200. He and his family eat about 100 bags a week, and in addition to keeping those, he also picks up any bags he finds in the street. Key's collection took up so much space in his shed that he now shrinks the empty packets with heat and then rolls them into tiny balls.

DIGITAL DIG

Robots have successfully navigated land, sea, and air. Now, burrowing soft bots are changing the way we explore the subterranean world. When creating this new technology, researchers at the Georgia Institute of Technology and UC Santa Barbara took inspiration from nature, from the way plants grow their roots into soil to how southern sand octopuses blast water into the seafloor to loosen the sand. Along with rapidly, precisely, and noninvasively exploring the underground here on Earth, these burrowing robots could have applications for extraterrestrial exploration, too!

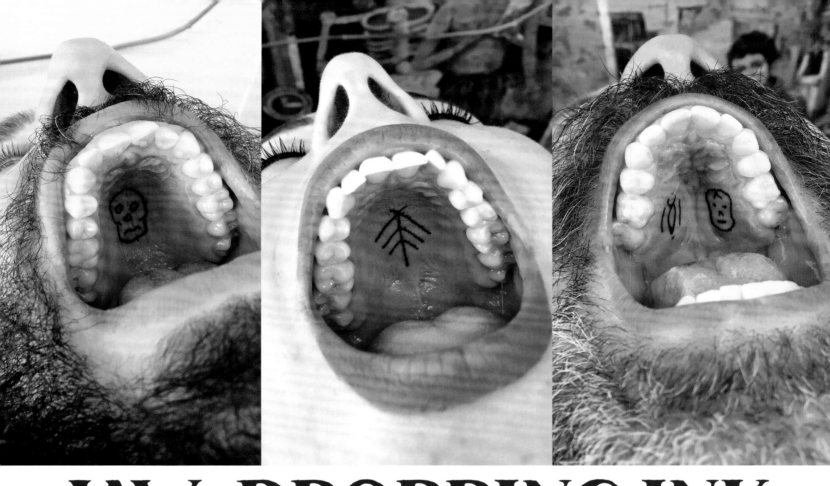

JAW-DROPPING INK

For genuinely jaw-dropping tattoos, look no further than the roof-of-the-mouth ink created by Belgian artist Indy Voet at the Purple Sun tattoo parlor in Brussels, Belgium.

Indy creates this inner-mouth art using the "hand poking" technique, which is basically just a single needle and ink. There are a couple of reasons for using this method. One is that there isn't enough room and maneuverability in such as small space. The other is because an electric tattoo machine would be too harsh for such a sensitive area of the body! Despite the bizarre placement, Indy claims that most of his clients feel little to no pain during the procedure.

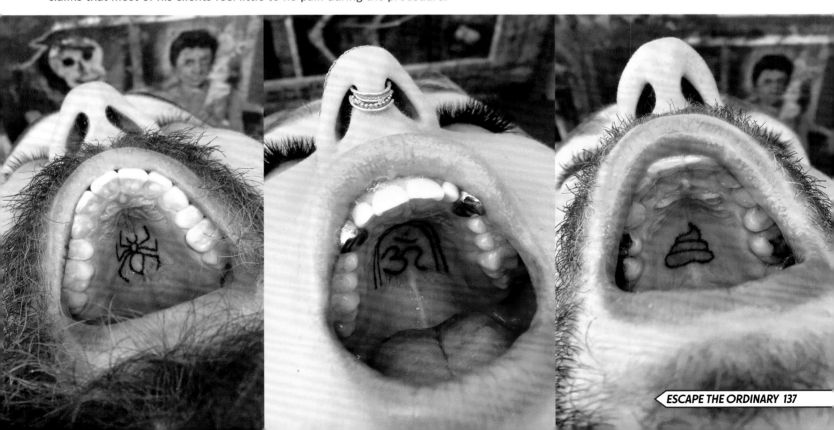

BALLOON BEASTS

Mark Verge, a.k.a. Jungle Jack, of Oshawa, Ontario, specializes in larger-than-life balloon sculptures that require thousands of inflatables to assemble!

He began twisting balloons about 30 years ago and has placed first in a dozen global competitions. Some of his incredible creations include a life-size car from *The Flintstones* (complete with Fred and Dino), Bumblebee from *Transformers*, Baymax of *Big Hero 6*, the titular characters from *Alien vs. Predator*, and so many more. However, Jungle Jack's most popular designs are his life-size dinosaur creations! His first prehistoric beast was a *T. rex* skeleton made of more than 1,400 balloons. It measured 39 feet (11.9 m) long and took 55 hours to create! Some of his other balloon dinos include *Triceratops*, *Stegosaurus*, *Utahraptor*, *Allosaurus*, and *Spinosaurus*.

MORE THAN 1,800 BALLOONS!

THE FLINTSTONES

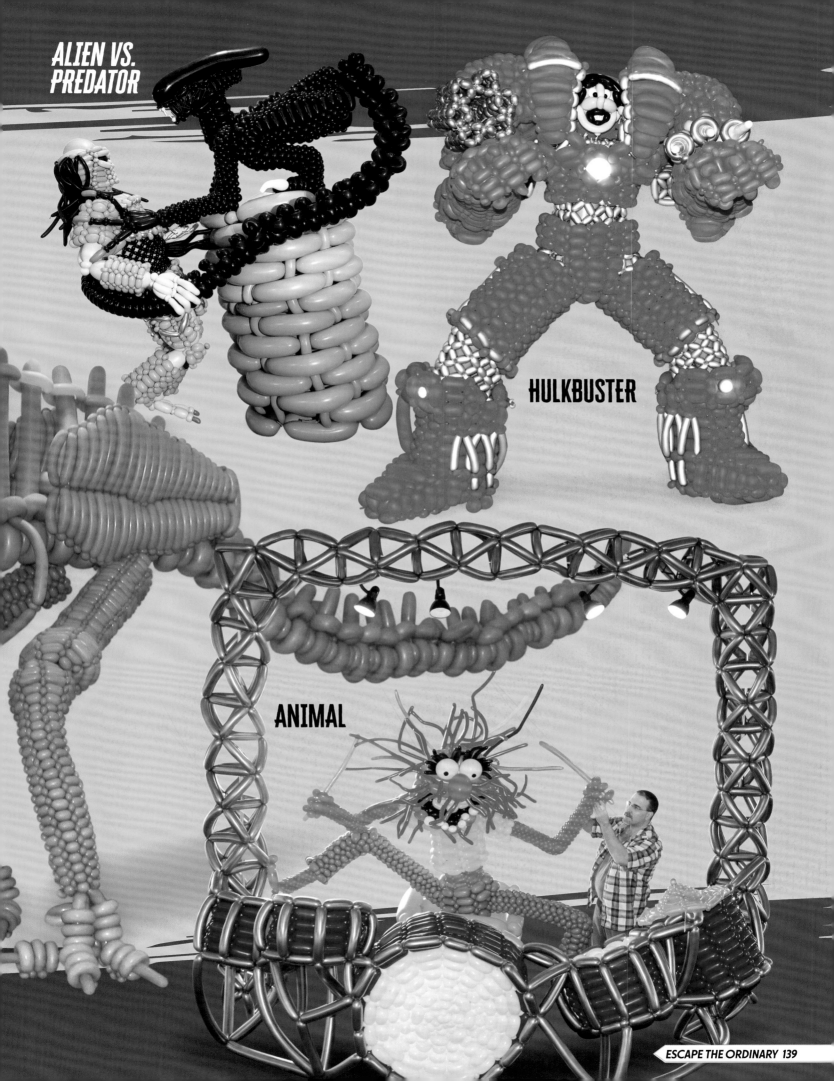

ALIEN VS. PREDATOR

HULKBUSTER

ANIMAL

KEEPING IT COOL

Believe it or not, the process of getting ice used to involve a lot more than just a quick trip to the kitchen! For decades, everyone's ice was harvested from frozen ponds and lakes.

It wasn't until the late 1800s that iceboxes became a common sight in home kitchens. But even then, there was no way to make your own ice at home; instead, it was delivered by an iceman. These workers would supply ice that had been cut out of frozen lakes, rivers, and ponds in up to 300-pound (136-kg) chunks—large enough to survive the journey to their end destination without completely melting. The ice would then be cut into more manageable sizes, which icemen would deliver door to door. Ice harvesting and delivery became relatively obsolete in the mid-1900s, once most homes had upgraded to electric refrigerators.

During World War I, women took over iceman delivery jobs.

STADIUM COOP
Darren Johnson, of North Texas, built an exact 1:60 scale model of the Houston Astrodome to serve as a coop for his chickens. It took him about 100 hours to build the coop, which features a Houston Astros baseball team logo, an American flag, and the numbers of all the retired jerseys. His chickens are all named after Astros players.

DYNAMITE CARVING
More than 90 percent of the carving on South Dakota's Mount Rushmore was done with dynamite. Chisels and jackhammers were tried first, but they were too slow at tackling the 450,000 tons of granite that needed to be removed in order to create the four presidential faces. Instead, powdermen placed charges of dynamite to blast away sections of rock with such precision that they were able to get within 3 to 6 inches (7.6 to 15.2 cm) of the final design.

HUMAN TUSKS
Rico Ledesma, a.k.a. Orc, a tattoo artist and body modification enthusiast from Iguatemi, Brazil, has had two giant false tusks implanted into his lower row of teeth so that he looks like a mythical orc from fantasy novels and games. He also has a split tongue, sliced ears, both eyes tattooed black, and eight subdermal piercings under his skin to look like horns. Roughly 80 percent of his body is inked.

SKATEBOARDING BULLDOG
Twice a week, Sonya, a five-year-old French bulldog, shows off her skateboarding skills at an indoor skate park in Chelyabinsk, Russia. She goes there with her owner, Dmitry, and uses one of her back legs to push off before standing with all four feet on the board while gliding along.

DELAYED DIPLOMA
After leaving high school prematurely in 1938 to help support his family, Albert Montella, of Media, Pennsylvania, was finally presented with his high school diploma in October 2020—just weeks before his 100th birthday.

HOCKEY MARATHON
Starting on February 4, 2021, a group of 40 sports enthusiasts in Edmonton, Alberta, Canada, traded shifts to play an outdoor hockey game that lasted 252 hours (more than 10 days)—even though the extreme cold caused pucks to shatter and sticks to break. The marathon game ended with a score of 2,649 to 2,528.

MOOD MUSIC
New Zealand's Department for Conservation hired a saxophonist to encourage endangered kakapo birds to breed by putting them in the mood for mating. The plan appeared to work because 76 chicks hatched in 2019—more than double that of previous years.

CAREER CRIERS
When it comes to "odd jobs," it's tough to beat the professional mourners of China. They adhere to traditional funeral rites dating back to the Han dynasty 2,000 years ago. Although the Chinese Communist Party banned professional mourners during the Cultural Revolution, these practices have since seen a significant rebound. In the process, a select group of performers has risen to the ranks of paid weepers, combining the best of age-old Chinese traditions with modern entertainment.

SCREAM THERAPY

In 2020, Iceland set up seven remote locations where people could vent their frustrations with life by recording their screams and hearing them played back over loudspeakers.

TREE WEDDING

The centerpiece of the annual Maggio di San Giuliano festival in Accettura, Italy, is a wedding between two trees. The groom, a male oak tree, is chopped down in a local forest and transported by 56 pairs of oxen to the town, where with the help of a hand pulley system, the bride, a female holly, is grafted onto its trunk.

19 YEARS

How long Australian squash player Heather McKay went without losing a single competitive match.

MANY EPISODES

The pop-culture news television show *Entertainment Tonight* has aired more than 12,500 episodes since it debuted in 1981. The program's 10,000th edition aired on January 10, 2020.

PROTECTIVE PEACOCK

When a duck made her nest in a planter in the patio area of the Rain Bar & Grill restaurant in Eugene, Oregon, she was protected by a local peacock, which hissed at anyone who got too close to the eggs.

SASHIMI STAMP

Hawaiian artist Naoki Hayashi is one of the foremost gyotaku artists in the world, and Ripley's is honored to have one of his pieces in our collection.

Before the invention of photography, anglers in Japan preserved records of their largest or most unusual catches by making inked reproductions known as *gyotaku*.

The word *gyotaku* translates as *gyo* "fish" and *taku* "rubbing." But this tradition soon developed into much more than a way to earn bragging rights. By the mid-nineteenth century, these pieces developed into veritable artwork as fishermen began embellishing their pieces with paintbrushes. They added details such as the color of scales or eyes, and even juxtaposed interesting groupings of marine life. Today, artists around the world continue the practice, even extending the artwork to other kinds of animals.

MUMMIES ON PARADE

In April 2021, a procession of 22 royal Egyptian mummies were moved between museums in Cairo using specially made airtight vehicles in a lavish event dubbed "The Pharaohs' Golden Parade."

The event marked their relocation from the Egyptian Museum to the National Museum of Egyptian Civilization in Al Fustat. The preserved pharaohs consisted of 18 kings and four queens from the seventeenth through twentieth dynasties. To protect the ancient bodies, they were transported in oxygen-free, nitrogen-filled boxes placed on vehicles decorated to look like boats the Egyptian rulers would have been carried on to their tombs. Notable ancients involved in the spectacle included Pharaoh Ramses II and Queen Hatshepsut.

SURF'S PUP!

As the world's only SURFice therapy dog, Ricochet helps children and adults with special needs experience salt life through assistive surfing.

Since the first time she caught a wave in 2009 with a quadriplegic boy named Patrick, she's gone on to hang ten (or rather, hang paws) with hundreds of first-time boarders of every capability. Some surfers rely on Ricochet to help keep them standing while others lie next to her. Either way, she keeps the board balanced, avoiding a wipeout and empowering riders every step of the way!

DINOSAUR BRAIN
Although the *Stegosaurus* grew up to 30 feet (9 m) long, 14 feet (4.3 m) tall and weighed nearly five tons, its brain was only the size and shape of a bent hot dog.

MISLEADING TITLE
Although known as the "king of the jungle," lions live chiefly in grassland. There is only one population of forest-dwelling lions in the world today—in India's Gir Forest National Park.

LUNAR CAMERAS
There are 12 Hasselblad cameras on the Moon, including the one that took the iconic picture of Neil Armstrong walking on the Moon's surface in 1969. The Swedish company designed the cameras specifically for NASA.

PRISON KEY
The 5-inch-long (13-cm) steel key to French emperor Napoleon Bonaparte's prison bedroom on the island of St. Helena in the South Atlantic, where he died in 1821, sold in 2021 at auction for £81,900 ($111,300 USD).

STATUE TRAGEDY
The body of a 39-year-old man was discovered inside the leg of a papier-mâché statue of a *Stegosaurus* in Barcelona, Spain. The police believe he dropped his phone down the statue's leg and became stuck headfirst when he tried to retrieve it.

TIRE SHOES
The first Doc Martens shoes were created from old tires. German doctor Klaus Maertens injured his foot while skiing in 1945 and used the tires to construct special soles that had air trapped within closed compartments, thereby cushioning his foot. They proved to be so successful that he launched them commercially two years later.

POP-UP RESTAURANTS
Four times a year, Finland celebrates Restaurant Day, when people are allowed to open a food stand, bar, café, or restaurant anywhere they choose in the country—at the roadside, in a park, in an office, in a garden, or on a rooftop.

Millions of live European chafer beetles washed up on a shore near Scarborough, Yorkshire, England, in April 2020, turning the whole beach gray.

NECK WRECK

A crash landing between two swans left one with its head lolling and neck spiraling sideways. The oddball swan was nicknamed "Wonky" by local wildlife officials. Although the swan's appearance shocked animal experts and passersby alike, he was given a clean bill of health by a veterinarian and returned to his flock.

OFF-LIMITS

For seasoned travelers, going somewhere most people will never see holds a certain allure, but there are some places even the most daring cannot visit.

In many cases, it's to protect people from extreme danger. Sometimes, it's to keep top-secret information away from prying eyes. And there are some places that are off-limits in order to preserve what lies within. Here are a handful of locations around the world that flat-out prohibit visitors.

VATICAN SECRET ARCHIVES

The Vatican Apostolic Archives in Vatican City contain some of Western civilization's most prized originals. But for those jonesing to see Martin Luther's official excommunication papers, good luck. Researchers must go through a rigorous application process to gain access to the 53 miles (85.3 km) of archives dating back to the Dark Ages.

NORTH SENTINEL ISLAND

North Sentinel Island, India, has a reputation for killing visitors. Or rather, the Sentinelese people inhabiting the island do. Since time immemorial, they've refused nearly all contact with the outside world at spear-point. So, the Indian government designated a 3-mile (4.8-km) restriction zone to keep non-islanders out.

SNAKE ISLAND

About 90 miles (144.8 km) off the coast of São Paulo, Brazil, sits Ilha da Queimada Grande. Also known as Snake Island, it is absolutely covered in golden lancehead vipers. Containing up to five snakes for every 10 square feet (0.9 sq m), the island was made off-limits to tourists by the Brazilian government. Considering the snake's venom dissolves human flesh, can you blame them?

FIRST EMPEROR'S MAUSOLEUM

The Tomb of the Qin Shi Huang remains one of the most remarkable archaeological discoveries of the twentieth century. An estimated 8,000 clay soldiers guard the emperor's tomb, with only 2,000 uncovered so far. Yet, the central chamber of China's first sovereign leader remains untouched, partially to protect its contents, but also out of fear of booby traps!

AREA 51

Rumored to contain the bodies of space aliens and the UFOs they flew in on, Nevada's Area 51 is strictly off-limits to civilians. Long before its existence was first reluctantly disclosed by the government in 2013, it has been in the crosshairs of curious citizens. Nevertheless, the only way in is with a security clearance on a private plane whose windows are drawn upon landing.

LASCAUX CAVES

If you think you can visit France's Lascaux Caves and see its famous prehistoric artwork up close, think again. The closest you'll ever get are reproductions. The original paintings, discovered in 1940, showed damage by the 1960s from carbon dioxide produced by visitors. So, the French government created replicas for the masses while barring general admission to the real deal.

COCA-COLA VAULT

The Coca-Cola Vault contains the brand's most highly guarded document: the original 1886 soda recipe. Kept under lock and key since the 1920s, few individuals have seen it. Nevertheless, you can visit Atlanta's World of Coca-Cola Museum, where the recipe rests, getting closer than ever before to the source of the bubbly mystery.

NEW PERSPECTIVES

UK artist Luke Jerram creates surreal scenes using massive, illuminated orbs of the Earth, Mars, and the Moon, measuring up to 33 feet (10 m) in diameter.

By relying on highly detailed NASA imagery, Luke recreates these celestial objects at an astonishing size. For example, his 23-foot-diameter (7-m) *Museum of the Moon* piece is at a scale of 1 to 500,000. That means every 1 inch (2.5 cm) of the orb is equal to almost 8 miles (12.8 km) of the actual lunar surface.

With his Earth orbs, Luke hopes to provide his audience with the "overview effect" experienced by astronauts, which instills people with "a profound understanding of the interconnection of all life, and a renewed sense of responsibility for taking care of the environment." If you stand about 690 feet (211 m) away from *Gaia*, it appears the same size as it would if you were looking at the real thing from the surface of the Moon. Talk about an out-of-this-world experience!

NOT-SO-PICKY EATER

While employed by the Zoological Society of London at the London Zoo, photographer Frederick William Bond had the opportunity to snap a shot of the contents of an ostrich's stomach around the year 1930. Taken after the bird's passing, Bond documented the aftermath of a voracious and indiscriminate diet. Items included a buttoned glove, two handkerchiefs, and a length of rope. But the metal objects in the animal's stomach, namely a 4-inch (10-cm) nail, ultimately led to its death. Also retrieved from its gizzard were metal tacks, hooks, staples, and copper coins.

ALLITERATIVE BOOK

Rapper Chris Elliott (a.k.a. The Real Frii), from New Haven, Connecticut, published a 724-word-long book of poetry, *The Epic Poem: Mastermind*, which features 340 words beginning with the letter "M" that do not repeat and are separated by three syllables or fewer.

QUEEN MOVIE

Joanne Connor of Brisbane, Australia, watched *Bohemian Rhapsody*, a 2018 movie about the rock band Queen, 108 times in theaters—equal to 10 days of nonstop viewing. She has also watched it more than 300 times at home—although she wasn't even a Queen fan before the movie was released.

OLD PERFUME

Perfumers Isabelle Ramsay-Brackstone and Jean Claude Delville recently created a limited edition scent, *Mary Celestia*, which was based on a 150-year-old bottle of fragrance found on the wreckage of a ship of the same name that sank in the late nineteenth century off the coast of Bermuda.

TREE GRAPES

The Brazilian jaboticaba tree grows fruit on its trunk! While more well-known fruits grow by dangling from a tree branch or vine, plants that exhibit cauliflory grow their fruits directly on the trunk. The jaboticaba's fruit resembles gigantic wild grapes, and in plentiful years, they may cover a tree from root to limb, claiming nearly every inch of its bark. These "tree grapes," as they are nicknamed, ferment quickly after being harvested, which is why you probably won't see them in your local grocery store any time soon.

FLOATING HIGH

Suspended 115 feet (35 m) above London's streets, you'll find the Sky Pool, an 82-foot-long (25-m) see-through swimming pool affording terrifying views of the ground below.

The acrylic water feature sits ten stories above the city, and it isn't for the faint of heart. Most terrifying of all, it stretches between two residential skyscrapers with views of the roadway below. If this pool sounds like an aquatic adventure you'd like to experience for yourself, keep in mind you'll need to become a resident of the EcoWorld Ballymore's Embassy Gardens development in southwest London's Nine Elms neighborhood.

GARBAGE GROTTO

The Cavern of Lost Souls in the Ceredigion region of Wales is an old slate mine that now acts as a rubbish dumpster and final repository for old cars.

The Cavern contains two large, accessible chambers. The central chamber measures 65 feet (19.8 m) deep, though largely flooded, with an opening to the surface. For decades, people have used this access point to dispose of everything from microwaves to televisions and even vehicles. Because of the vibrant turquoise color of the millpond's still water and the single ray of light that illuminates the Cavern, it could be called one of the most strikingly photogenic "dumpsters" in the world.

HOUSE OF MUGS

In Collettsville, North Carolina, a residence exudes coziness with a mug-covered façade just begging visitors to stop for coffee or tea. Created by Avery and Doris Sisk, the couple's obsession with these hot beverage souvenirs began after Avery purchased 15 and decided to showcase them on the exterior walls of their house. Fifteen years later, the couple welcomes guests to add a mug to their abode (if they can find a nail).

SOLOMON'S CASTLE

Located in the tiny town of Ona, Florida, Solomon's Castle is the ultimate "dreamed turned reality" for Howard Solomon. Although he died in 2016, his architectural fantasy remains—a testament to his colorful and eclectic legacy. The castle is constructed from aluminum printing plates, and the grounds include a replica of a Portuguese galleon, an on-site restaurant, and a souvenir shop.

NINE BABIES

Halima Cissé, a woman in her mid-20s from Mali, gave birth to nonuplets in 2021. Her five girls and four boys—two more babies than doctors had detected during scans—were born by cesarean section.

MARRIAGE TRIALS

Every four years, the village of Great Dunmow in Essex, England, awards a flitch (a side) of bacon to married couples from anywhere in the world who can convince a judge and a jury of 12 unmarried people that they have not had a major argument for a year and a day. The festival is known as the Dunmow Flitch Trials and dates back to at least the fourteenth century.

FREE WI-FI

A Swiss couple gave their baby daughter the second middle name Twifia—after internet provider Twifi—in order to win 18 years of free Wi-Fi.

DISAPPEARING WATERFALL

On February 2, 2020, a massive sinkhole caused Ecuador's biggest waterfall—the 492-foot-high (150-m) San Rafael Waterfall—to disappear overnight. The sinkhole opened up right before the falls on the Coca River in the Amazon rainforest and diverted the gushing flow into three small streams, reducing the waterfall, which had been there for thousands of years, to a trickle.

SWALLOWED BUD

Brad Gauthier of Worcester, Massachusetts, had surgery to remove an AirPod from his esophagus after he had accidentally swallowed it in his sleep. He had woken to find one of the wireless earbuds was missing, and when he tried to drink some water but could not swallow, he went to a hospital—where doctors discovered the reason for his discomfort.

SECRET SISTERS

Cassandra Madison and Julia Tinetti met in 2013 when they were both working at the Russian Lady Bar in New Haven, Connecticut. They became friends and eight years later discovered they are biological sisters.

TIME PYRAMID

The German village of Wemding is home to a concrete pyramid that will not be finished for another 1,160 years. Work on the *Time Pyramid* began in 1993 at the suggestion of local artist Manfred Laber to commemorate the 1,200th anniversary of the village's founding, with a plan to lay one block every decade until the year 3183. By 2021, the first three of its 120 blocks had been put in place.

HANGING CAGES

Still hanging from the steeple of St. Lambert's Church in Münster, Germany, are three empty iron cages that 500 years ago contained the mutilated, rotten corpses of religious revolutionaries led by John of Leiden. He and two others were tortured and executed in 1536, and their bodies were hung in the cages, where they remained as a deterrent for 50 years.

STOMP AND CHOMP

While they might have the menacing appearance of portable torture devices, these nineteenth-century clogs had a truly innocent purpose. Found in the Hautes Ardèches region of Auvergne, France, they were actually used to crush chestnuts! Worn by peasants, they were essential to food production, but today they instill terror at first glance.

DRESSED TO IMPRESS

The term *pulgas vestidas* sounds rather fancy, even though its translation of "dressed fleas" leaves something to be desired. Even so, these masterpieces bring in thousands of dollars at auction today.

The art of costuming fleas and placing them in tiny dioramas likely began in the convents of Guanajuato, Mexico. Originally a commoner's craft, these tableaus soon gained enough interest to become popular tourist souvenirs. As the art became lucrative, the complexity of the pieces rose to impressive heights. *Pulgas vestidas* may include little more than a flea or two in costume, or they may be much larger, featuring full mariachi bands or even elaborate wedding processions!

ACTUAL SIZE!
→

Ripley's Exhibit
Cat. No. 168424

SAMURAI ARMOR

A 23-piece set of armor for a Japanese samurai warrior. Constructed of iron and leather, this ensemble is tied together with colorful silk cords and is meant to fit loosely on the wearer, allowing for a wide range of motion. Samurai followed a code of honor known as bushidō, which includes eight virtues: justice, courage, mercy, politeness, honesty, honor, loyalty, and self-control.

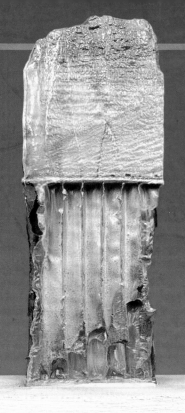

APOLLO 12 HEAT SHIELD

Apollo 12 was the second manned mission to the Moon. In order to safely return the astronauts to Earth, the command module was protected by a heat shield, which helped absorb high temperatures caused by immense friction the spacecraft experienced when reentering the Earth's atmosphere. Unlike the insulating tiles that were used on space shuttles later on, this shield was meant to vaporize under the intense heat of reentry.

APOLLO 12
HEAT SHIELD CORE
NOV 14/24, 1969

LEATHER FOOTBALL HELMET

The first documented case of a football helmet being used in an American football game was in 1893—24 years after the birth of the sport! Before players wore helmets with face braces, impact indicator chin straps, and air pads, most players wore a simple leather cap like this one—if anything at all. It wasn't until 1943 that the National Football League required all players to wear helmets.

CELERY
FLAVOR

NEW

for salads
JELL·O
BRAND

K

NET WT. 3 OZ.   salad gelatin mix

LIGHT DESSERT

Artist Leanne Rodriguez (a.k.a. Elrod) of Oakland, California, creates retro Jell-O–inspired artwork that doubles as functional decor!

Thankfully, none of her work contains actual food; Elrod makes her realistic pieces out of plastic castings and sculpted clay. These quirky lamps and clocks evoke the homey, sometimes nausea-inducing, vintage Jell-O recipes of the mid-twentieth century, complete with green olives and slices of meat and fruit suspended within translucent, multicolored layers of simulated dessert.

LIGHTS OUT!

LEANNE RODRIGUEZ "ELROD"

NOT FOR EATING!

EYES ON THE SKIES

The paradise tree snake lives in the forests of South and Southeast Asia, where it's gained a reputation for "flying" by launching off branches to attack prey. How far can these snakes glide through the air? It all depends on the elevation they start at. Jake Socha, a researcher at Virginia Tech who has studied the animals for nearly 25 years, once witnessed a snake take the plunge from 30 feet (9 m) above the forest floor, catching air for about 70 feet (21 m)!

WATCH OUT FOR FLYING SNAKES!

$350 SANDWICH

Chicago, Illinois, restaurant PB&J sells a peanut butter and jelly sandwich that costs $350. Called "The Golden Goose," it features bread with gold dust baked into the flour, an edible gold leaf topping, and exclusive seedless redcurrant jam imported from France. It is also drizzled with rare Manuka honey from New Zealand.

POOP POWER

The BAP *Puno*, a 150-year-old Peruvian Navy steamship operating on Lake Titicaca, is fueled with dried llama dung.

STICKY FALLS

The Bua Thong Waterfalls in Thailand are also known as the "Sticky Waterfalls" because the rocks are covered with a mineral deposit that gives them extra grip and makes them feel like a hard sponge. Since no algae or slime clings to the rocks, it is possible to climb the almost vertical waterfalls with bare hands and feet without ever slipping.

BRIDGE HOUSE

A tiny home is located in the middle of a four-lane highway bridge in Guangzhou, China. For 10 years the house owner, Ms. Liang, refused to be relocated, so the builders constructed the Haizhuyong Bridge around her home with two lanes running on each side.

WHIRLWIND WEDDINGS

A Taiwanese bank employee married the same woman four times and divorced her three times in the space of 37 days in 2020—just so that he could qualify for extended paid leave from work. Under Taiwanese law, workers get eight days of paid leave when they marry, so he quickly amassed 32 days by repeatedly divorcing his wife and remarrying her the next day.

NASAL COIN

A 59-year-old man from Zelenograd, Russia, experienced breathing problems for more than half a century because he had shoved a metal coin up his nose when he was six and had then forgotten all about it. When he eventually had problems breathing through his right nostril, doctors discovered and removed a very old one-kopeck coin.

NUTTY SQUIRREL

After a four-day trip, Bill Fischer of Fargo, North Dakota, returned home to discover a squirrel had transformed his truck into a winter food pantry stuffed with black walnuts. Just how many did the little guy pack in during Bill's absence? While cleaning his Chevy, Bill recovered 42 gallons of nuts!

BIRD SONG

When imagining the sounds of a city, many people's first thoughts are the hum of traffic, the thud of construction, or loud conversations. But in old Beijing, China, the sound of the city included pigeon whistles!

Made from hollowed-out gourds or bamboo, these small instruments were tied to the tail feathers of a pigeon. When the bird flew, the wind would create a musical note. Whole flocks could be fitted with whistles, creating what famous Peking opera singer Mei Lanfang once called "a symphony in the sky." The origin of pigeon whistles is said to go back about 900 years, when they were used for military communication. Nowadays, the modern sounds of the city drown them out, and only a few people continue to make the instruments.

SCORCHED SUMMIT

Every January, locals in Japan light the dry grasses and brush of Mount Wakakusa on fire during the Wakakusa Yamayaki, or Wakakusa Burning Mountain, Festival.

The 1,122-foot-high (342-m) hill sits in the Nara Prefecture, and no one knows exactly how the annual blaze got started, but locals have practiced the tradition for hundreds of years. Some claim the festival serves a practical purpose in driving wild boars and pests from the area. Others believe it stems from a boundary dispute between two of the most prominent temples of Nara. Either way, the stunning, smoldering sight attracts tourists worldwide.

RAINBOW ROCKS

On the western side of Glacier National Park in Montana, you'll find Lake McDonald and its Instagram-worthy rainbow pebbles. How did such a plethora of colors end up in one location? Different rock hues formed during different eras. Over time, rock fragments of each tint eroded away, washing downstream into streams and rivers. Water erosion smoothed and polished the pebbles, which eventually made their way into the lake, creating a vast, multi-hued waterscape.

OUT OF WATER

Francis McEachern, of Montreal, Quebec, made an incredible catch after noticing a perfect fish pattern in a maple tree stump getting removed after a windstorm. Francis couldn't believe his luck (or his eyes) as he angled landscapers into letting him take the fishy image home. Despite receiving multiple offers from woodworkers and novelty collectors interested in acquiring the finned silhouette, Francis decided to keep the oddity for himself.

BEATLES LYRICS

Paul McCartney's 1968 handwritten lyrics for the Beatles' "Hey Jude" sold for $910,000 in 2020. McCartney had jotted down the lyrics on a sheet of paper before a recording session in London and later gave it to a studio engineer.

LOST HAT

While working in Belle Chasse, Louisiana, in 2015, Matthew Bonnette accidentally dropped his customized purple and gold hard hat into the Mississippi River. The hat was mailed back to him five years later after being found 4,300 miles (6,920 km) away on a beach in County Clare, Ireland.

GREAT SURVIVOR

King Zog I of Albania survived a staggering 55 assassination attempts. He eventually died at age 65 in 1961 of an unspecified condition, possibly as a result of his habit of smoking 200 cigarettes a day.

HUMAN CALCULATOR

Using an educational math app, 10-year-old Nadub Gill, from Derbyshire, England, solved 196 multiplication and division questions in one minute, averaging more than three correct answers per second.

VIDEO PROPHECY

In 2010, actor Chris Pratt shot a behind-the-scenes video for the TV show *Parks and Recreation* in which he joked that Steven Spielberg was texting him about a role in *Jurassic Park 4*. Five years later, Pratt starred in *Jurassic World*, the fourth installment of the Jurassic Park film series.

RELAY RUN

Setting off on April 15, 2020, 48 runners from the 5,000 Mile Run Club completed a continuous relay of just over 5,055 miles (8,088 km) around an athletics track at Northern Guilford High School in Greensboro, North Carolina, in 26 days.

RUBIK MOSAIC

Nine-year-old Benjamin Russo, from Montreal, Canada, built a giant mosaic of the face of wrestler and actor John Cena with 750 Rubik's Cubes. Benjamin has dyslexia, which he describes not as his disability but as his superpower.

MOUTHWATERING MINERALS

Most of us stopped putting rocks in our mouths sometime in early childhood, but some crystals and minerals look so appetizing you might think twice.

At a bare minimum, you'll do a double take, shocked by the stunning similarity of certain geological formations to foods we eat every day. From malachite to rhodochrosite, here are some of nature's most delectable-looking crystals and minerals.

SUMMER STONE

Watermelon tourmaline is a mouthwatering gemstone with a green outer layer like a rind and a deep pink or reddish center like a juicy watermelon. But watch out for imitation versions of this popular stone. Authentic watermelon tourmaline features a fade between colors, whereas fake versions have crisp lines.

BACON BITS

Rhodochrosite is known as the "bacon of gemstones," and with good reason. An ore of manganese, this incredible stone contains stunning brown, red, pink, and white banding reminiscent of breakfast's favorite pork treat. Of course, you won't get the savory smell or salty good flavor. Nevertheless, that appearance still exudes artery-clogging deliciousness.

HARD CANDY

Nothing appears more delectable than fudge-colored calcite hematite, the geologist's equivalent of a deconstructed chocolate bar. The microscopic hematite grains in the rock contain deep brown crystals, lending it that tempting, Hershey-like allure.

FINGER LICKIN' GOOD

For the rockhound with a hankering for fried chicken, there's this red calcite specimen that bears a striking resemblance to a fried chicken finger. What gives it the gold breaded exterior and white meat center? A calcium carbonate mixture of aragonite and calcite.

NO YOLK

Just when you thought it couldn't get any weirder, there's yellow botryoidal fluorite, which looks like a fried egg sunny side up. These rare specimens get their Waffle House good looks from a yellow globe of fluorite perched atop a bed of pale amethyst crystals.

WINE NOT

Delicious clumps of botryoidal purple chalcedony make for another forbidden food: table grapes that'll never shrivel into raisins. Formed by tiny quartz crystals with a botryoidal (which actually means "grape-like") clustered appearance, they range in shade from lavender to deep purple and look ready for the winepress.

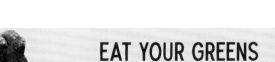

EAT YOUR GREENS

A vibrant copper mineral mined worldwide, malachite comes in brilliant shades of green. It can have a rough, textured, clumpy surface that looks uncannily like florets of broccoli. But these rocky eats are anything but Green Giant approved.

MEDICAL STUDY

In 1994, the same year that *Friends* debuted, Lisa Kudrow co-authored the medical paper "Handedness and Headache," which appeared in the neurological journal *Cephalalgia*. Her father, Dr. Lee Kudrow, founded the California Medical Clinic for Headache and she worked for him for eight years, earning a research credit on his study into the relationship between cluster headaches and left-handedness.

MASH SCULPTURES

For over a decade of family Thanksgiving dinners, Greg Milano, of West Haven, Connecticut, has been carving miniature sculptures out of mashed potatoes. He uses a butter knife to create his "mash-terpieces," which include intricate models of Stonehenge, the White House, a DeLorean car, LEGO characters, the Guggenheim Museum, and Tesla's electric Cybertruck. After finishing each model, he heats it up, douses it in gravy, and eats it.

KOALA RESCUE

Since being employed by the organization Detection Dogs for Conservation, Bear, an Australian Koolie dog that was abandoned as a pet, has rescued more than 100 sick, injured, or starving koalas following the bushfires in 2020 and 2021. He sniffs the koalas out and when he finds one, he sits down next to it and waits for his handler.

BACKWARD INTRO

The intro to Eddie Floyd's 1967 song "Knock on Wood" is the same as the intro to the 1965 tune "In the Midnight Hour" by Wilson Pickett—but played backward! Both intros were written by guitarist Steve Cropper, who simply decided to reverse the chord progression to make them sound different.

SCENIC SINKHOLE

In late May 2021, a massive sinkhole opened up in Santa María Zacatepec, Mexico, becoming something of a local tourist attraction. The hole grew to a width larger than a football field, swallowed a house, destroyed farmland, and trapped two dogs on a ledge. Fortunately, the dogs were rescued and received care from local veterinarians. Large groups began gathering around the natural disaster, prompting the deployment of local soldiers to keep people a safe distance from the expanding hole, which had a 60-foot (18.3-m) drop into the water. Scientists hypothesize the cause of the sinkhole may have been an underground river.

FAN FEED

OKRA POD ART

This fan submission will make you rethink your relationship with okra. Instead of boiling, frying, or pickling the green veggies as most folks do, Kathy Tate Davis creates whimsical ornaments and sculptures using the pods. Kathy started making the one-of-a-kind vegetable art in 1993. Over the years, her designs have become increasingly elaborate. They include intricate Santa Claus, frog, and hen sculptures requiring large numbers of pods, and sometimes even pinecones!

MEGA MARIONETTE

The 2020 Tokyo Nippon Festival, which ended up taking place in Japan's Tohoku region in 2021, featured a sight of epic proportions: a 33-foot-tall (10-m) puppet known as MOCCO.

The puppet is operated like a marionette, except instead of hanging from and being controlled by a single hand, MOCCO hangs from a crane and is operated by multiple people. The giant doll is partially crafted from fabrics that represent the Tohoku region's six prefectures. After making its initial appearance in Tohoku, the giant puppet toured the nation, bringing smiles to locals and helping build a sense of community following the tenth anniversary of the Great East Japan earthquake.

TWEET TREAT

In July 2020, researchers on Frégate Island in the Seychelles witnessed a giant tortoise deliberately hunting prey! Deputy Conservation Manager Anna Zora filmed the bizarre event, watching nature take course as the tortoise followed a hopping tern chick too young to fly, before the reptile finally caught up and snatched the bird in its jaws. Although the giant herbivores are known to eat non-vegetable foods such as leftover bones and discarded eggs, none had ever been caught on camera gobbling a baby bird, representing a grisly first for these otherwise gentle giants.

COOKIE RUSH

Lilly Bumpus, an eight-year-old cancer survivor, sold 32,484 boxes of Girl Scout cookies outside her San Bernardino, California, home in a single season.

DUCK CLEANERS

Every year in Thailand, thousands of young ducks are released to clean the rice fields of pests and to remove the stubble left behind from the harvest. As well as clearing snails and weeds, the ducks fertilize the fields with their poop. A flock of 10,000 ducks can clean up a 173-acre (70-hectare) farm in a week.

TALL HAIR

Joseph Grisamore, of Park Rapids, Minnesota, has a full mohawk hairstyle that stands an incredible 42.6 inches (108.2 cm) tall. It took him seven years to grow it to that height, and he achieves the look with the help of half a can of hair spray.

STICKER BALL

Vermont company Sticky Brand Creative Group made a giant sticker ball that measured 7.1 feet (2.2 m) in circumference and weighed over 308 pounds (140 kg). The ball was made up of 250,000 recycled stickers.

HIGH PASS

On April 24, 2021, NFL star Rob Gronkowski caught a football dropped from a helicopter 600 feet (183 m) above the ground at the University of Arizona stadium in Tucson.

DEEP BREATH

Budimir Buda Šobat held his breath underwater for 24 minutes 33 seconds at a swimming pool in Sisak, Croatia.

JUGGLING SWIMMER

Bob Evans, a teacher at Pacific Ridge Elementary School, Oregon, completed 101 catches straight at a pool in Seaside while swimming and juggling five balls—a pursuit known as "swuggling." He has also completed 224 catches while swuggling with four balls.

7,000 HOMES

The approximate number of homes in the UK that still have a black-and-white TV set.

Ripley's—*Believe It or Not!*®

CIRQUE DU SEWER

Instead of elephants and clowns, Melissa Arleth is revamping the concept of a circus by featuring the perfect furry assistants: cats and rats!

Melissa's animals are all rescues, and they travel the country with her to perform at various fairs and festivals under the name Cirque du Sewer. Some of the stunts her feline and rodent costars can do include balancing acts, jumping through flaming hoops, and racing through obstacle courses. Besides the cute antics of her creatures, Melissa also performs slack rope walking, acrobatics, juggling, and more.

SHIP SHAPE

Tony DeMatteo of Churchville, New York, constructed two 50-foot-long (15.2-m) pirate ships in his front yard to celebrate Halloween 2021.

The self-proclaimed Halloween enthusiast has spent the past five years outdoing himself each October with displays that continue to increase in production value and size. Known locally as "Halloween on Ambush," the decorations attract thousands of visitors each year, many of whom donate to local causes of Tony's choosing. The 2021 display helped raise $6,000 for Golisano Children's Hospital Pediatric Intensive Care Unit, plus 1,800 pounds (817 kg) of food and nearly $1,000 to Open Door Mission of Rochester, New York.

The maritime-themed scene was Tony's most ambitious undertaking to date. It included cannon effects, a light show at night, and even handmade kraken tentacles attacking one of the ships! To create his annual masterpieces, Tony starts between eight and 10 months in advance. This project required 5,000 feet (1,524 m) of cabling in the front yard and even included visitations by professional actors playing the roles of Captain Jack Sparrow and Captain Barbossa.

LEGENDARY LOG

A vertical log known as "The Old Man of the Lake" has been bobbing around Oregon's Crater Lake for more than 120 years, traveling up to 3.8 miles (6.1 km) a day. You can spot about 3 feet (0.9 m) of the tree above the water, but like an iceberg, most of its 30-foot (9.1-m) height is hidden below the surface. Its presence was first recorded in 1896; however, carbon dating puts the stump at about 450 years old. How the Old Man remains vertical is a mystery, and there are some who believe it controls the weather at Crater Lake (a theory bolstered by a string of storms that occurred after the Old Man was tied up for research in 1988).

FLOATING UPRIGHT FOR MORE THAN 100 YEARS!

MOBILE ALLEY

Businessman Terence Jackson Jr., from Detroit, Michigan, converted a semi-trailer truck into a mobile bowling alley. The alley features two 25-foot-long (7.6-m) lanes, neon lighting, a digital scoring system, automatic ball return, and automatic pin-resetters. The balls are smaller and lighter than in regulation bowling, being about the size of grapefruits and without any holes.

STAR STARER

Anh Tran Tan from Vietnam has about 600,000 followers on TikTok even though most of his video posts are him doing nothing but stare expressionlessly into his smartphone camera. One of his uploads has been viewed over 50 million times.

FLORAL TEDDY

A 2021 wedding vow renewal ceremony for 108 couples in Wanning City, China, was watched over by a 20.1-foot-tall (6.1-m), 7-ton teddy bear made from 48,000 red roses attached to a wire frame.

DEADLY BOOK

Shadows From the Walls of Death, an 1874 book by U.S. author Dr. Robert M. Kedzie, contained samples of arsenic-pigmented wallpaper and was considered so dangerous that it could kill a careless reader. He had 100 books produced as a warning of the dangers of such decorations because about 65 percent of all wallpaper in U.S. homes at the time contained arsenic. He distributed the book to public libraries across Michigan with a note to librarians telling them not to let children touch the pages.

MOON DUST

Moon dust is so sharp it can cut right through astronauts' space suits! This is because it is mostly composed of very fine particles of silicon dioxide glass. On the Apollo 17 mission in 1972, lunar dust wore through three layers of Kevlar-type armor on astronaut Harrison Schmitt's boot.

PIGEON MESSAGE

While hiking in northeastern France in 2020, Jade Halaoui found a 110-year-old carrier pigeon message. He spotted a 2-inch-long (5-cm) aluminum cylinder half-buried in the ground and upon investigating discovered that it contained a piece of paper written by a German infantry officer and dated either 1910 or 1916. The message had probably slipped from the leg of the pigeon that was supposed to deliver it.

SEVERED FINGER

Until recently, when a member of Papua New Guinea's Dani tribe died, women from the tribe would cut off part of one of their fingers to satisfy ancestral ghosts. The severed portion was then burned and the ashes stored in a safe place.

DRIP 'N' SIP

When conditions are just right, caves can create tubular formations known as "soda straws."

Stalactites—cave formations that hang from the ceiling—grow in areas where water slowly leaks between rocks and deposits minerals over thousands of years. The types of minerals, the flow of the water, and many other variables determine what shape stalactites will take. For soda straws to form, calcium sulfate or calcium carbonate suspended in water droplets is deposited at the edge of the droplet before it falls to the ground. As each drop is replaced by a new one, the process repeats, resulting in what the name suggests: rock formations that look like plastic soda straws!

START: BOBBY PIN

2. Earrings

3. Margarita glasses

4. Vacuum cleaner

6. Apple TV 4K

8. Xbox One, with accessories

5. Beginner snowboard

10. Canon T6, with accessories

7. Bose wireless headphones

12. Nike Hyperdunks

9. 2011 MacBook Pro

11. Nike Blazers

14. Apple iPhone 11 Pro Max

13. Nike Air Jordan 1s

15. 2008 Dodge Grand Caravan

RIPLEY'S EXCLUSIVE

BIG DEAL

Demi Skipper of San Francisco, California, successfully bartered her way from a single bobby pin to an entire house!

Starting in May 2020, Demi documented her incredible journey from hair accessory to home on TikTok, where she garnered millions of followers curious to see if she could reach her goal. Less than two years later in November 2021, she made her final trade: a solar-powered trailer for a house in Clarksville, Tennessee! Inspired by the process, she decided to renovate the house and give it to a deserving individual in exchange for—believe it or not—another bobby pin! As she started her adventure anew, Ripley's spoke with Demi to find out what it was like turning a bobby pin worth $0.01 into an $80,000 house.

Q: What inspired you to begin your bartering journey?
A: In May of 2020, I saw a video about a man named Kyle MacDonald who traded a red paperclip all the way up to a house about 20 years ago and was immediately inspired. I knew I had to be the next person to do it!

Q: Which item were you most surprised to receive in a trade?
A: I think the trade where I really realized that my trading journey was going to work was when I traded an old snowboard for an Apple TV. It was my first electronic and also my first Apple product. I was so excited.

Q: Were there any items you wanted to keep?
A: I traded four cars in total throughout the journey, and I actually don't have a car of my own. I was always tempted to keep the cars, but knew that I had to keep my eye on the prize and get all the way to the house!

Q: Which item was the most difficult to trade?
A: At one point, I had a $40,000 trailer that was in Canada. It took me almost five months to get the trailer from Canada back in the U.S. because

END: HOUSE!

of the borders being closed. I worked with border patrol and the trailer's manufacturers almost every day to successfully get it into the U.S.

Q: Was there ever a point when you considered giving up?
A: There were definitely times that were difficult. Especially when the trades didn't end up in my favor. In those moments, I never considered giving up, but I had days where I needed to take a step back and remember why I started this journey.

Q: What advice do you have for people who want to try this?
A: Be ready to be told "No." For every 100 people I messaged about a possible trade, 99 of them would say "no" until I got my first yes. It's all about being determined to find that one person who needs what you have and is willing to make a trade.

Also, know the item you have. For every new item you have to trade, make sure you learn everything you can about it, including its value and who would be interested in it! That way, you get the best trade possible.

16. Boosted Plus electric skateboard

17. Newer Macbook Pro

18. Ferla food cart bike

19. 2006 MINI Cooper Convertible

20. Diamond and sapphire necklace

21. Peloton stationary bike

22. 2006 Ford Mustang GT Deluxe

23. 2011 Jeep Patriot Sport

24. Wildbound tiny cabin

25. 2011 Honda CRV

26. Three tractors

27. Chipotle VIP Burrito Card

28. Solar-powered trailer

Ripley's®
UP CLOSE &
PECULIAR

Ripley's Exhibit
Cat. No. 10129

BONE FLUTE

One of the oldest instruments in Tibet is the bone trumpet, also known as a *kangling*. This one is made from a human thigh bone. It is not uncommon in Tibetan Buddhist culture to turn body parts into ceremonial or spiritual items. The kangling is said to have a haunting sound.

INCREDIBLE HEALING POWERS!

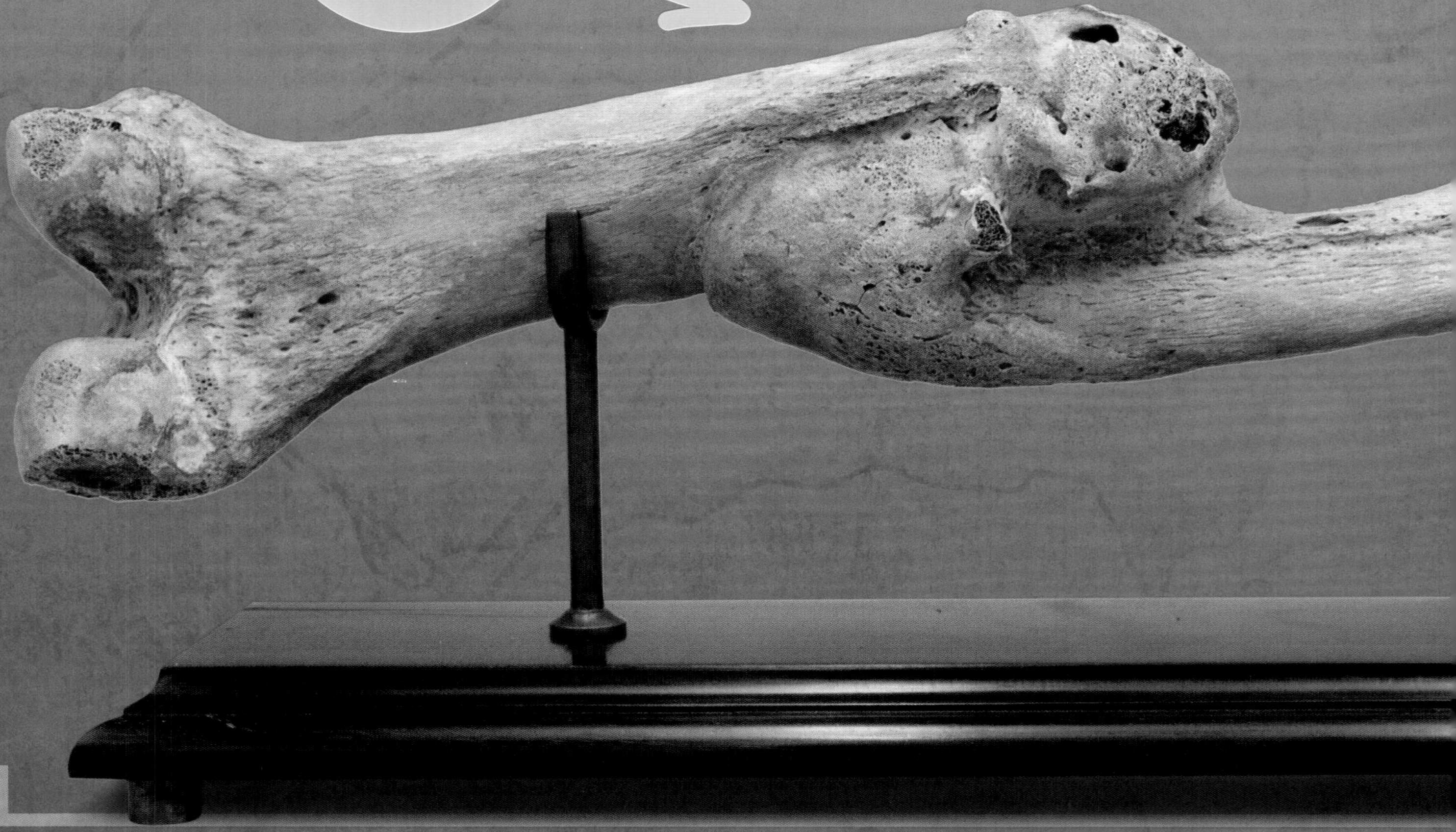

Ripley's—**Believe It or Not!®**

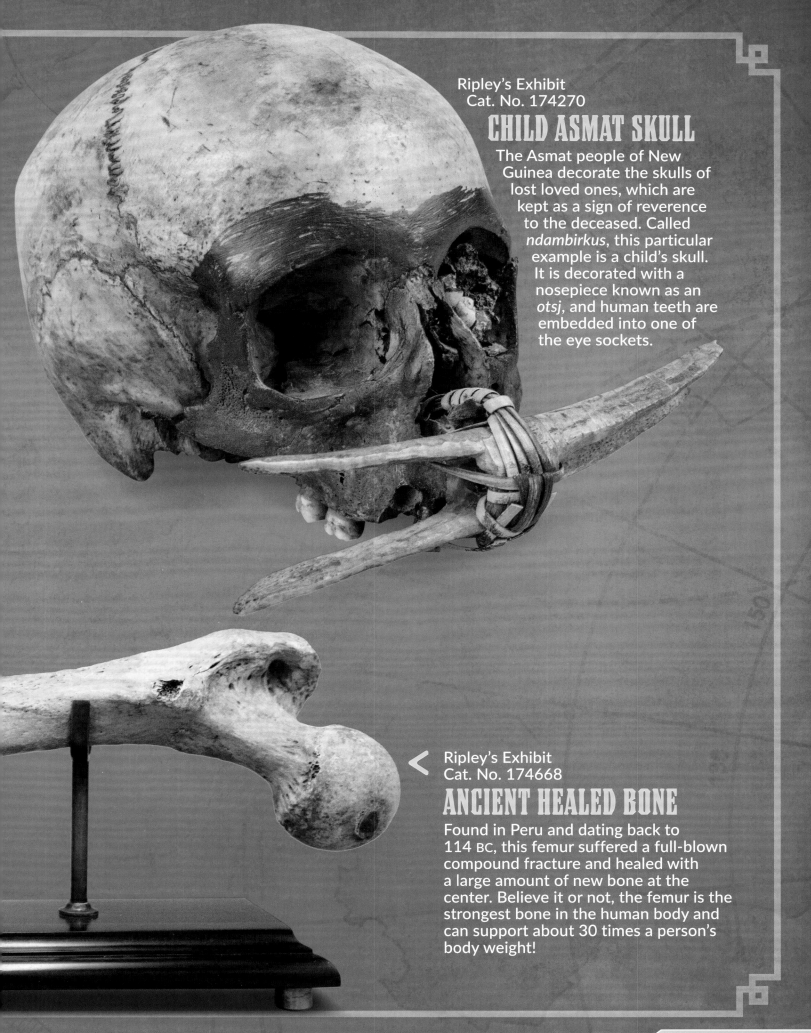

CHILD ASMAT SKULL

The Asmat people of New Guinea decorate the skulls of lost loved ones, which are kept as a sign of reverence to the deceased. Called *ndambirkus*, this particular example is a child's skull. It is decorated with a nosepiece known as an *otsj*, and human teeth are embedded into one of the eye sockets.

ANCIENT HEALED BONE

Found in Peru and dating back to 114 BC, this femur suffered a full-blown compound fracture and healed with a large amount of new bone at the center. Believe it or not, the femur is the strongest bone in the human body and can support about 30 times a person's body weight!

HANGING BY A THREAD

Extreme athlete Stefanie Millinger performed an aerial hoop routine while hanging from a ski gondola at a stomach-churning height— without any safety equipment!

The feat took place in picturesque Vorarlberg, Austria, at the Hotel Jägeralpe. When extreme athletes perform without protective gear—such as a rock climber not using a rope or harness— it is known as "free soloing." While many

"When I am doing free-solo stunts, I am focused and the senses are sharpened to the maximum."

UNDEAD ORCHESTRA

The Covent Garden Sinfonia orchestra debuted a tribute concert to *The Walking Dead* in August 2021, featuring a 22-piece ensemble of classical musicians who performed in zombie special-effects makeup. To complete the look, performers dressed in ripped and aged evening gowns and tuxedos. All told, SFX artists spent more than eight hours transforming the players into the undead, complete with cutting-edge prosthetics.

ROOF RACE

From 1923 to 1982, the Fiat Lingotto Factory in Turin, Italy, churned out Fiat automobiles and tested them on a rooftop track!

Cars were assembled starting at the bottom of the factory and worked their way up to the roof, where they were driven for the first time. Although the Lingotto building now houses a shopping mall and hotels, you can still visit the racetrack where the 1969 film *The Italian Job* filmed its famous car chase scene with Michael Caine. Today, you'll find a garden on-site, and if you care to take a spin, keep in mind only electric vehicles are permitted on the track.

POTTY PEDAL

In October 2020, cyclist Ruben Lopez completed a 2,500-mile (4,023-km) journey between Poo Poo Point, Washington, and Pee Pee Creek, Ohio, to raise awareness and money for the humanitarian crisis in Yemen. Despite the silly nature of his trip, he's raised more than $11,000 in aid.

BROADWAY VERSION
In 1902, 37 years before the Judy Garland film, a stage production of *The Wizard of Oz* debuted in Chicago, then ran for 293 performances on Broadway. The show had 60 songs, had no appearance by the Wicked Witch of the West, and instead of Toto the dog there was a cow named Imogene.

AIR GUITAR
More than 3,700 people played air guitar to AC/DC's "Highway to Hell" at the 2020 Perth Festival in Western Australia.

BEE CAST
About 22 million bees were employed for the 1978 horror movie *The Swarm*. Around 800,000 of the insects had their stingers carefully removed so that the actors could work safely with them, with the result that only one cast member, Olivia de Havilland, was stung during the production.

ICONIC LAUGH
To create SpongeBob SquarePants's distinctive laugh, Tom Kenny repeatedly taps his throat with his hand right above his Adam's apple while saying "Ahh."

HEIGHT DIFFERENCE
Because Gillian Anderson is 10 inches (25 cm) shorter than her *X-Files* costar David Duchovny, for many of their scenes together she stood on an apple box.

LION PASSENGER
While still at school, former *Doctor Who* actor Jon Pertwee used to ride a motorcycle around the Wall of Death in a circus with a real lion in the sidecar.

ALTERNATE TITLE
Ringo Starr wanted the Beatles's *Revolver* album to be called *After Geography* because the Rolling Stones had recently released an album called *Aftermath*!

Nepal has the only national flag in the world that is not a quadrilateral. Instead of being a square or rectangle, it is in the shape of two triangular pennants, one above the other.

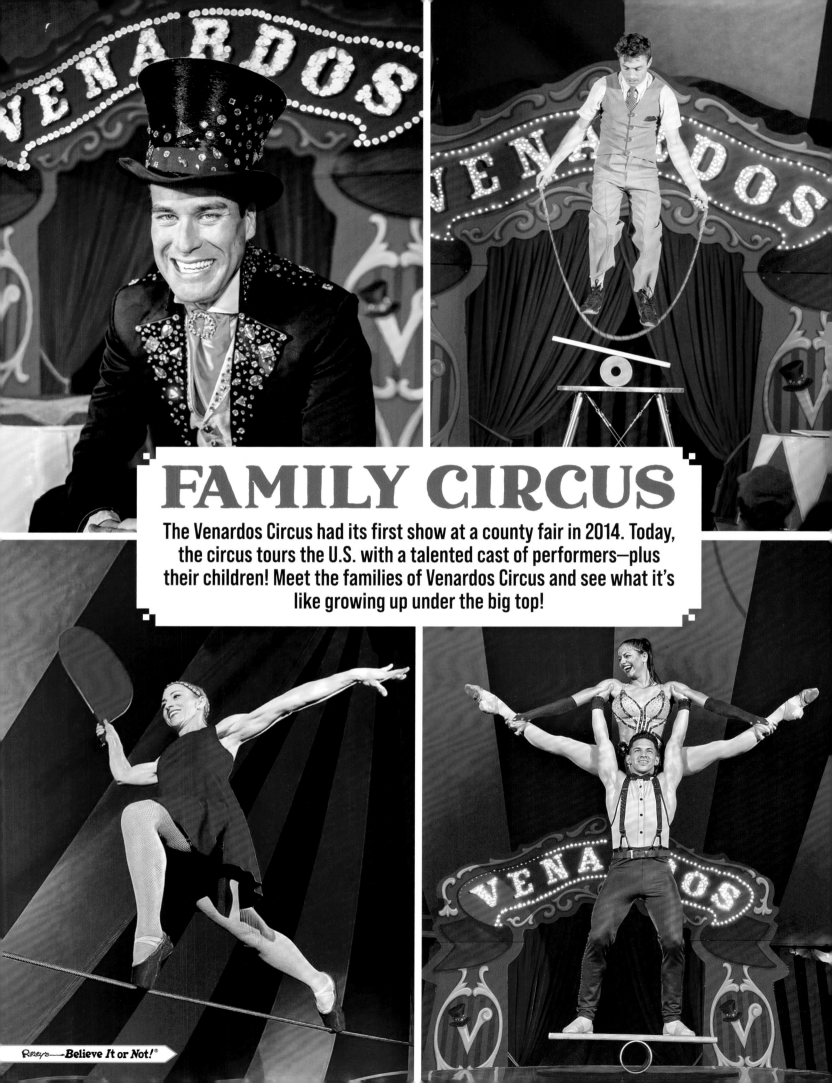

FAMILY CIRCUS

The Venardos Circus had its first show at a county fair in 2014. Today, the circus tours the U.S. with a talented cast of performers—plus their children! Meet the families of Venardos Circus and see what it's like growing up under the big top!

JUGGLING ACT

Ariele Ebacher walks the tightrope on the tips of her toes in pointe shoes! Meanwhile, her husband Jann Damm jumps rope while balancing on the rolla bolla!

Ariele and Jann have been performing together since they met at a show in 2011. They married in 2016 and today they have two children, five-year-old Timo and three-year-old Ilsa, who have become part of their parents' acts. Timo clowns around with his dad in a comedic musical chairs act, and Ilsa helps her mom by bringing Ariele her pointe shoes for her highwire finale! The little ones often steal the show, to their parents' delight, and through the circus are learning anything is possible.

STAYING FLEXIBLE

Husband-and-wife team Manuel and Ilenay Acosta perform mind-bending acrobatics and body-bending acts of contortion together on stage, including their exhilarating Chinese pole routine! The dynamic duo met at circus school in 2007, have toured the world together, and are now married with two kids. For one-year-old Derek and four-year-old Daphne, hanging out backstage surrounded by circus performers is nothing new. In fact, when most babies are just learning to walk, Derek is confidently standing in his father's hand, balancing as Manuel carefully lifts him high off the ground!

MASTER MINDS

As his name implies, Kevin Venardos is the founder and ringmaster of Venardos Circus. Having previously worked with Ringling Bros. and Barnum & Bailey Circus, one of the largest traveling circuses of all time, Kevin sought to create a more intimate circus experience. Now, he and his family live on the road as Venardos Circus tours the country. Believe it or not, Kevin is not the only master at this circus! His partner, Marianne Eaves, was the first female master bourbon distiller in Kentucky, and she continues to operate a mobile lab to blend her signature spirits. On top of all this, Kevin and Marianne are raising their two young daughters, Andi Lane and Billie Mae.

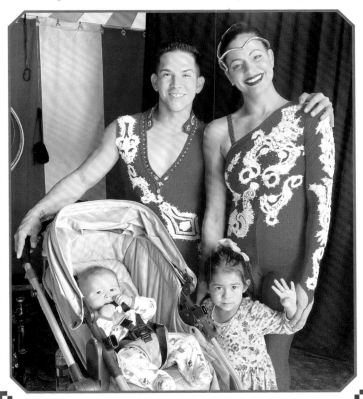

SAND SURPRISE

Believe it or not, about 70 percent of the sand on beaches in Hawaii and the Caribbean are made of parrotfish poop!

Around the globe, parrotfish swim in shallow subtropical and tropical waters grazing on algae that smother coral reefs. While scraping algae from reefs with their beak-like teeth, parrotfish often eat chunks of coral, too. Tooth plates in their throats known as "pharyngeal mills" help grind up these pieces into grains small enough for the fish to digest. The grains are pooped out, *et voilà*—new sand!

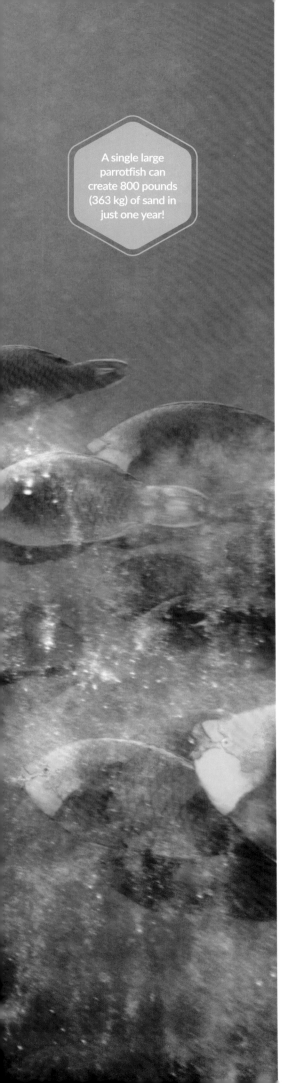

A single large parrotfish can create 800 pounds (363 kg) of sand in just one year!

STINKY STANDS

While you're probably familiar with the smelly spraying antics of striped skunks, their smaller, polka-dotted cousins have added a twist to the defense mechanism. In one quick movement, spotted skunks will perform a handstand as a final warning before spraying potential threats. They'll even walk towards predators in this position, balancing on their front paws! Native to North America, these little stinkers seem unaware of their small stature. Despite weighing in at just 2 pounds (0.9 kg), they've been spotted facing off against mountain lions!

BEAR DELAY

A Siberian Airlines passenger flight attempting to land at an airport in Magadan, Russia, on August 17, 2020, was delayed for 20 minutes because there was a bear on the runway.

45,000 HOLES

Over a period of three years, Nguyen Hung Cuong, an artist from Hanoi, Vietnam, drilled 45,863 holes—most of them smaller than the width of a human hair—into a single, hollowed-out ostrich egg.

When Swedish-Italian ballerina Marie Taglioni gave her final performance in St. Petersburg, Russia, in 1842, some of her fans bought her old shoes, cooked them in a stew, and ate them.

MAD MONTH

In just 30 days, 63-year-old Arvid Loewen, from Winnipeg, Manitoba, Canada, rode his bicycle more than 450 times to Lockport and back, covering a total distance of more than 7,000 miles (11,265 km).

STICK REMOVED

While cleaning the teeth of eight-year-old rescue dog Buddy, a veterinarian from St. Petersburg, Florida, removed a stick that had been wedged between two teeth in the dog's mouth for at least three years.

DEATH SMELL

Aristolochia microstoma, a plant native to Greece, emits the smell of dead beetles in order to attract one of its chief pollinators, the coffin fly.

BROWN CHEESE

Brunost, the most popular cheese in Norway, is brown. It is usually sliced very thinly and has a distinctive caramel flavor. It is made from whey—the liquid left after the milk has been curdled and strained during the cheese-making process. A mixture of milk, cream, and whey is boiled for several hours so that the water evaporates. The heat turns the milk sugars into caramel, giving brunost its unusual color.

CHRISTMAS BANNED

Christmas was once banned in Massachusetts for 22 years. When the Puritans settled there in 1659, they banned the holiday because they were fearful of its pagan origins and introduced a five-shilling fine for anyone caught celebrating it. The unpopular law was finally repealed in 1681.

NO FEAR

To cure Jody Smith, from New York City, of his epileptic seizures, doctors removed part of his brain, including the amygdala, the section responsible for how a person reacts to danger. As a result, he no longer feels fear.

LOST MONEY

More than £200,000 in passengers' lost coins and bills is found on public transportation in London, England, in an average year.

POOP WALL

In 2020, a farmer in Lodi Township, Michigan, built a 250-foot-long (76-m) wall made of cow dung to separate his land from a neighboring property.

99 STEPS

When getting married at the Bled Church of the Assumption, which is located on an island in Lake Bled, Slovenia, it is tradition for the groom to carry his bride up the 99 steps that lead to the church.

VERTICAL DROP

Mount Thor on Canada's Baffin Island is 5,495 feet (1,675 m) tall—but that includes a sheer, vertical drop of 4,101 feet (1,250 m). Made of granite, the mountain's unusual shape is a result of it being cut in half by glacial erosion during the last Ice Age over 20,000 years ago.

NO MILITARY

Located between France and Spain, the small country of Andorra has no official military—just a ceremonial army made up of about 12 volunteers whose main role is to present the national flag at official events.

DINO DIAL

The Tyrannophone contains a real *T. rex* tooth fragment that's 80 million years old! Created by luxury smartphone modifier Caviar, only seven of the customized iPhone 13 Pros were created, costing $8,160 each. The focal point is a raised image of a *Tyrannosaurus* with real gold lightning flashing above its head. Pure amber gives its eye a flashy yellow glint, and the tooth fragment sits within the menacing rows of fangs. The limited-edition phone is part the brand's "Tera" collection, which also includes a nearly $50,000 diamond-encrusted case.

REAL
T. REX
TOOTH!

RETURN TO NATURE

Artist Dan Rawlings of Gloucestershire, England, transforms vehicles into intricate nature scenes using a freehand plasma cutter.

One such work is entitled *Future Returns*, in which the steel shell of an oil tanker was cut into a forest canopy, complete with delicate, intertwined limbs and foliage. Dan uses a plasma cutter to "draw" with extreme heat, melting the metal of his vehicular canvases. The tanker was exhibited in a nineteenth-century church in Lincolnshire, England, and is meant to inspire spectators to examine the role they play in changes to the environment.

THE FUTURE IS NOW

Despite getting further from *Back to the Future Part II's* 2015 setting every day, recent advancements are getting us closer to that iconic vision of a future with flying cars.

The brainchild of Professor Stefan Klein, the AirCar takes little more than two minutes to transform from road-ready to cloud-ready. Powered by standard gasoline and a BMW engine, this hybrid aircraft-car can fly approximately 600 miles (966 km) at a height of 8,200 feet (2,500 m). In tests, it has remained airborne for upward of 40 hours. It may be a while before your average driver is able to take to the skies at the push of a button, but developments like the AirCar put us on the road to a future where, as Doc Brown said, "We don't need roads."

PORTAL CONNECTION

In a move to make people rethink what it means to be united, two cities in Eastern Europe have connected via giant circular screens. The "portals" allow people to peer into a city more than 250 miles (400 km) away in real time—and have someone look back, almost like a giant webcam or video call! To check out this sci-fi tech for yourself, you'll need to travel to Vilnius, Lithuania, or Lublin, Poland, where the cutting-edge spherical communication devices stand.

TURN BACK TIME

Observant people visiting the historic Plaza Murillo in La Paz, Bolivia, will do a double take upon seeing the unique clock perched atop the House of Congress thanks to the fact that it runs backward and counterclockwise! Known as the "Clock of the South," the one-of-a-kind timekeeping device is said to pay homage to the nation's two main indigenous peoples: Quechua and Aymara. In both of these groups' languages, the future is referred to as being behind you, while the past lies ahead.

FOOD FIGHTERS

While it might sound great to nosh on delicious food to your heart's content, competitive eating is no walk in the park.

It requires strenuous training to stretch your stomach, and the bathroom aftermath can be, well, *overwhelming*. Not to mention the choking hazards. In other words, don't try to replicate the feats below at home! Like most professional sporting events, competitive eating contests keep ambulances on standby for a reason.

MATT STONIE

Today's McDonald's Happy Meals include a cheeseburger, fries, a soda, and healthy sides like apple slices. While competitive eater Matt Stonie didn't opt for the apples, he downed the burger, fries, and soda in just 15.22 seconds! Matt remains the unlikely prince of competitive eating, despite weighing just 130 pounds (13.6 kg).

JOEY CHESTNUT

Joey "Jaws" Chestnut of Westfield, Indiana, remains one of the greatest competitive eaters of all time. Not only does he exhibit an extraordinary talent for stomaching hefty loads, he's also versatile when it comes to various foodstuffs. On July 4, 2021, he downed 76 Nathan's Famous hot dogs and buns in 10 minutes.

MOLLY SCHUYLER

In July 2021, Molly Schuyler, a mother of four from California, tied for the win in Washington's Z-Burger twelfth annual "Independence Burger Eating Championship." Molly downed 34 hamburgers in 10 minutes, as did her fellow competitive eater Dan "Killer" Kennedy of Pennsylvania.

MIKI SUDO

Miki Sudo of Las Vegas, Nevada, continues to astound competitive eating fans with her voracious appetite. At the Prairie Farms World Ice Cream Eating Championship in Indianapolis, Indiana, she swallowed 16.5 pints of ice cream in 6 minutes. Talk about a brain freeze!

DARRON BREEDEN

Competitive eating is synonymous with Darron Breeden. One of the most famous professional eaters nationwide, he's completed feats like eating 43 hot dogs and buns in ten minutes. But the record he's most proud of? Devouring 48 Oreos and half a gallon of milk in a mere 2 minutes 28 seconds.

MIKE JACK

Mike Jack, from London, Ontario, Canada, ate three Carolina Reaper peppers—the hottest peppers in the world—in under 10 seconds. The Carolina Reaper is 820 times more potent than a jalapeño pepper and measures more than 1.6 million on the Scoville heat scale on average, but can get as hot as 2.2 million Scoville heat units!

NICK WEHRY

Nick Wehry entered the competitive eating circuit in 2017 after 11 years as a competitive bodybuilder. On April 25, 2021, he set a world record for consuming hardboiled eggs. How many did Nick eat? He stunned those watching by downing 50 eggs in just 3 minutes 2 seconds.

SCANNING MAKES MUSIC!

BARCODE-BOARDING

Japanese experimental music group Electronicos Fantasticos has devised a way to turn a skateboarder's moves into music with their Barcode-Boarding project.

Led by Ei Wada in collaboration with the Kitakyushu Skateboard Association, this electromagnetic style of skateboarding relies on a barcode scanner attached to a skateboard. The scanner reads striped patterns on the ground and translates them into different sounds. Skateboarders are able to achieve a variety of audio effects depending on how fast they go and which design they ride over.

BARCODE-BOARDING

FLORAL TRIBUTE

Every May 19 since 1850, a basket of red roses has been sent to the Tower of London where Anne Boleyn was beheaded in 1536 on the orders of her husband, King Henry VIII. Mystery surrounded the sender for 150 years until it was revealed to possibly be Anne's descendants in Kent, England, who now have the surname Bullen.

EMPTY CHAIR

When Jade Dodd, of Hickman County, Tennessee, received her new driver's license in the mail, her ID card showed a photo of an empty chair instead of her face. The Department of Motor Vehicles said the wrong picture had been saved to Dodd's profile.

BLOOD CANDY

A nutritional candy bar widely sold in Russia and other parts of Eastern Europe contains real blood. The Hematogen bar, a chewy snack with a metallic aftertaste that is especially popular with children, features about five percent processed cow's blood.

COUPONS ONLY

Hiroto Kiritani from Japan has been living almost exclusively on coupons for more than 35 years. He regularly acquires coupons and vouchers for food, clothing, the gym, and the movie theater. He only spends real money on utilities and rent.

ON A ROLL

Since the 1960s, Grantchester, England, has held an annual barrel-rolling relay race on Boxing Day. The race involves pushing barrels along a 100-yard course at top speeds. Participants compete in small teams of four, and part of the trick remains moving the barrels as fast as possible without harming any of the hundreds of spectators standing by.

EYE OF THE TIGER

British wildlife photographer Paul Goldstein has run more than 20 marathons while wearing a 10-foot-tall (3-m) Bengal tiger suit. As part of his "Worth More Alive" campaign, Paul has competed in events ranging from the Brighton and London Marathons to the challenging Everest Marathon in Nepal. Paul competes in these races to highlight the plight of tigers in the wild and has raised hundreds of thousands of dollars to support the conservation efforts of India's Bandhavgarh National Park.

SKIN DESIGNS
Emma Aldenryd, a student from Aarhus, Denmark, has dermatographia, a skin condition that causes her skin to swell up and redden when touched. So, Aldenryd creates her own body art by running a pencil over her skin to form temporary designs that fade 30 minutes later.

DOMINO EFFECT
Red Cedar Elementary School in Bluffton, South Carolina, toppled 3,730 cereal boxes like dominoes in a chain reaction.

UNOPENED GAME
A rare unopened and still-sealed copy of the 1986 video game *Super Mario Bros.* sold for $660,000 at a Texas auction in 2021.

EMUS BANNED
Gerry and Chris Gimblett, the owners of the Yaraka Hotel in Queensland, Australia, banned the town's resident emus, Kevin and Carol, from the premises after they kept stealing food. The birds had learned to climb the front steps and would even snatch bread from the toaster.

SWALLOWED STICK
Rocky, a nine-month-old puppy, survived despite swallowing a stick that was half the length of his body. The 10-inch-long (25-cm) stick was removed in an hour-long emergency operation at an animal hospital in Southampton, England.

OFFICE ALPACA
A video production in Wuxi, China, hired a young huarizo—a cross between a male llama and female alpaca—to walk around the office, helping employees relax and relieve stress.

MOUNTAIN MUMMIES

Although most people think of Egypt when they hear the word "mummy," the Anga people of Papua New Guinea have a unique process for mummifying their ancestors, and it involves smoking the dead.

Sources vary when it comes to how the practice began, but mummies can still be seen today, seated in wooden cages affixed to cliffsides and mountainous areas overlooking the villages where their descendants live. Successful mummification starts with removing moisture from the corpses by cutting slits in the joints and stomach and then inserting bamboo poles to encourage liquid drain-off. Bodies are then smoked and dried in a special hut for a minimum of 30 days. Next, they get smothered in a red clay containing iron oxide that protects the flesh from the elements and scavengers. At this point, the mummies are ready for display, and they make the arduous journey to the cliffs above.

MYSTERY EGGS
A 62-year-old female ball python at St. Louis Zoo in Missouri laid a clutch of seven eggs in 2020—even though it was at least 15 years since she last had contact with a male.

LIVE TURTLE
Biologists at the Florida Fish and Wildlife Conservation Commission discovered a live turtle in the stomach of a largemouth bass that they had caught for research. After being excavated from the fish's innards, the turtle was released back into the water.

BMX WHEELIE
On August 27, 2020, BMX rider Max Ganakovsky, of Calgary, Alberta, Canada, achieved a 2,126-foot (648-m) manual—a wheelie trick where the rider is not allowed to pedal while the wheel is off the ground. He managed to keep his front wheel off the ground for just under two minutes.

ORIGAMI DOGS
Danilo Schwarz and Meire Matayoshi, from São Paulo, Brazil, spent 60 days making 1,010 origami paper dogs.

NEW MOM
Mangayamma Yaramati, from Andhra Pradesh, India, gave birth to twin baby girls in September 2019 at age 73.

SKIN CASE
A team of French and English researchers have developed a cell phone case that looks and feels like human skin. The case even responds to gestures such as tickling, punching, and caressing. For example, if the user tickles the accessory, it releases a laughing emoji onto the phone.

Ripley's Exhibit
Cat. No. 175211

LONGEST NAILS

Ayanna Williams of Houston, Texas, spent about 30 years growing her fingernails to a combined length of 24 feet 0.7 inches (733.55 cm)!

Since 2017, Ayanna held the Guinness World Records™ title of Longest Fingernails on a Pair of Hands (Female). That is, until she decided to memorialize them in a Ripley's Believe It or Not! Odditorium!

For Ayanna, it was bittersweet to part with her iconic nails. They were in her life for decades, and she enjoyed children's positive reactions to them. However, the extreme length made day-to-day activities difficult, and it took Ayanna a few days and up to four bottles of polish to paint her nails. At the dramatic clipping—which required the use of a Dremel tool—Ayanna quipped, "With or without my nails, I will still be the queen. My nails don't make me, I make my nails!"

Ripley's Exhibit
Cat. No. 175243
LONGEST HAIR

Nilanshi Patel of Modasa, Gujarat, India, stopped cutting her hair when she was six years old, allowing it to grow to an impressive length of 6 feet 6.7 inches (200 cm)!

This feat earned her the Guinness World Records™ title for Longest Hair on a Teenager. As she approached adulthood, she decided it was time for a new 'do and contributed her locks to Ripley's Believe It or Not!

At its longest, Nilanshi's hair just grazed the ground when dry. However, once wet—as it must be for official record measurements—her natural waves straightened, achieving that record-breaking length. "My hair gave me a lot," said Nilanshi at her first haircut in 12 years, "Because of my hair I am known as the 'real life Rapunzel', now it's time to give back." Inspired by her daughter, Nilanshi's mother donated a portion of her own long hair to cancer patients.

BUTCHER BIRD

The shrike, or "butcher bird," impales the bodies of its prey on the thorns of bushes or on the spikes of barbed-wire fences.

This not only makes it easier for the predatory songbird to tear the flesh into small, bite-sized pieces; it also provides a place to store food for later consumption. The shrike's victims include lizards, large insects, small rodents, and even other birds! This "leftovers" strategy even enables the shrike to eat toxic lubber grasshoppers, which only become safe to digest two days after death.

CATCH OF THE DAY!

ELUSIVE BEAR

A brown bear nicknamed Papillon escaped from a nature park in Trento, northern Italy, by climbing four fences, including a 13-foot-tall (4-m) electric barrier with seven wires charged at 7,000 volts, and then remained on the loose for 10 months before finally being caught. He broke free again in July 2020, that time going missing for 42 days before being recaptured.

MAIL CATS

In 1879, the Belgian city of Liège conducted a short-lived experiment using cats to deliver mail from the central post office to outlying villages. The letters were put into waterproof bags that were tied around the collars of 37 trained domestic cats, but the animals proved slow and unreliable, with some taking more than a day to reach their destination while others simply didn't bother.

270 DEGREES

How far rabbits can rotate their ears to detect sounds from up to 2 miles (3.2 km) away in almost every direction.

SLOTH POOP

Moths from South America in the *Cryptoses* genus live in the thick fur of sloths. The female moths wait until their host sloth comes down from the trees to defecate and then lay their eggs in its fresh poop. The caterpillars grow and develop in the poop, and when the adult moths emerge, they fly up into the trees to live in the sloths' fur, beginning the cycle all over again.

CYCLOPS PUPPY

A puppy owned by Somjai Phummaman and his wife Amphan, of Chachoengsao, Thailand, was born with only one eye—in the middle of his face. The mutant Aspin mix pup, nicknamed Kevin after the one-eyed *Minions* character, also had enlarged lips and had to be bottle-fed. Mah, the other puppy in the litter, was born without any abnormalities.

DEADLY JEWELRY

Writer Susan Prior of Australia's Norfolk Island spotted a mullet swimming around with a gold wedding ring around its neck! A little online research turned up a story of a man who had recently lost his gold wedding band at the beach. Sadly, this wasn't the first time Susan observed man-made objects causing harm to local fish. Susan has also seen many fish with plastic collars from milk and juice bottles slowly suffocating them. The bands end up around the fish as they sniff the seafloor for food. Susan reminds everyone to snip plastic rings before throwing them away, to avoid entangling creatures in trash.

LAVA SLICE

Chef David Garcia relies on an unconventional cooking method for his signature pizzas: the intense heat of Guatemala's Pacaya Volcano! Mastering the pizza craft with volcanic rocks was somewhat tricky, according to David. Facing temperatures up to 2,000°F (1,093°C), he must stay vigilant so he isn't hurt—and to keep the pizza from burning. But David says the risk is well worth it, as the technique imparts "an exclusive taste and an amazing crunch."

GLOBAL BIKER
Twenty-three-year-old Jack Groves, from Hertfordshire, England, spent nearly two years circumnavigating the world on a motorbike, traveling 35,000 miles (56,327 km). He set off in the summer of 2019, but his journey was delayed when he contracted COVID-19 in Peru and spent 255 days in quarantine.

LAKE JUMPER
To relieve stress during the COVID-19 pandemic, Chicago bus driver Dan O'Conor jumped into Lake Michigan every day for a whole year—365 days straight. In the winter, he often had to hack a hole in the ice on the frozen lake to make an opening big enough for him to jump through.

WATERMELON CRUSH
Las Vegas, Nevada, bodybuilder Kortney Olson can crush three watermelons with her thighs in 7.5 seconds.

110 MARATHONS
Gary McKee completed a 26.2-mile (42-km) marathon circuit around his home in Cumbria, England, every day for 110 consecutive days.

BAY RESCUE
Off-duty lifeguard Anthony Capuano saved the driver of an SUV that was sinking in Newark Bay, New Jersey, by taking off his prosthetic leg, jumping into the water, swimming out to the vehicle, and dragging the 68-year-old man back to shore. Capuano wears an artificial leg following an accident from more than a decade ago.

PAPER BIRDS
Evelyne Chia, of Colchester, England, folded 1,000 origami paper crane birds in 9 hours 31 minutes without taking any breaks.

SENIOR INSTRUCTOR
Takishima Mika works as a fitness instructor at a gym in Japan at age 90. Every morning before breakfast, she goes for a 2.5-mile (4-km) walk, followed by a 1.8-mile (3-km) jog and a 0.6-mile (1-km) backward walk.

UNICYCLE RIDE
On September 19, 2020, at Emmen, Switzerland, Mirjam Lips rode a unicycle for 62.5 miles (100 km) in a time of 3 hours 45 minutes 53 seconds.

WACKY WEBSITE
Devised by Swedish duo Oskar Sundberg and Per Stenius, the website eelslap.com allows you to virtually slap a man across the face with an eel just by moving your mouse.

SNEAKER COLLECTOR
Richard Hastings, of Bristol, England, has a collection of 500 pairs of sneakers. He always buys two pairs—one to wear and one to keep—and once waited in line for five days to obtain a pair he especially wanted.

GRAINY WEATHER

In the right conditions, sand can flow over rocks and cliffsides much like a waterfall.

These aptly named "sandfalls" can be as small as the water flowing from your bathroom sink or as large as an actual waterfall. They are typically caused by an outside force, such as wind or other movement, that triggers an avalanche-like reaction.

POKÉ-MALL

On the roof of the Songjiang INCITY mall in Shanghai, China, sits a 33-foot-tall (10-m) statue of Pikachu!

In fact, the entire mall is Pokémon-themed! Pikachu is joined by a giant Mew floating above the mall's entrance. Inside you'll find the smiling faces of Squirtle, Bulbasaur, Charmander, and other Pokémon on the glass sides of the escalators, plus photo-ops galore and even a human claw machine for snatching up Poké Balls! Fans of other franchises such as Harry Potter, Game of Thrones, and Marvel will be happy to know that these too will also make appearances at INCITY.

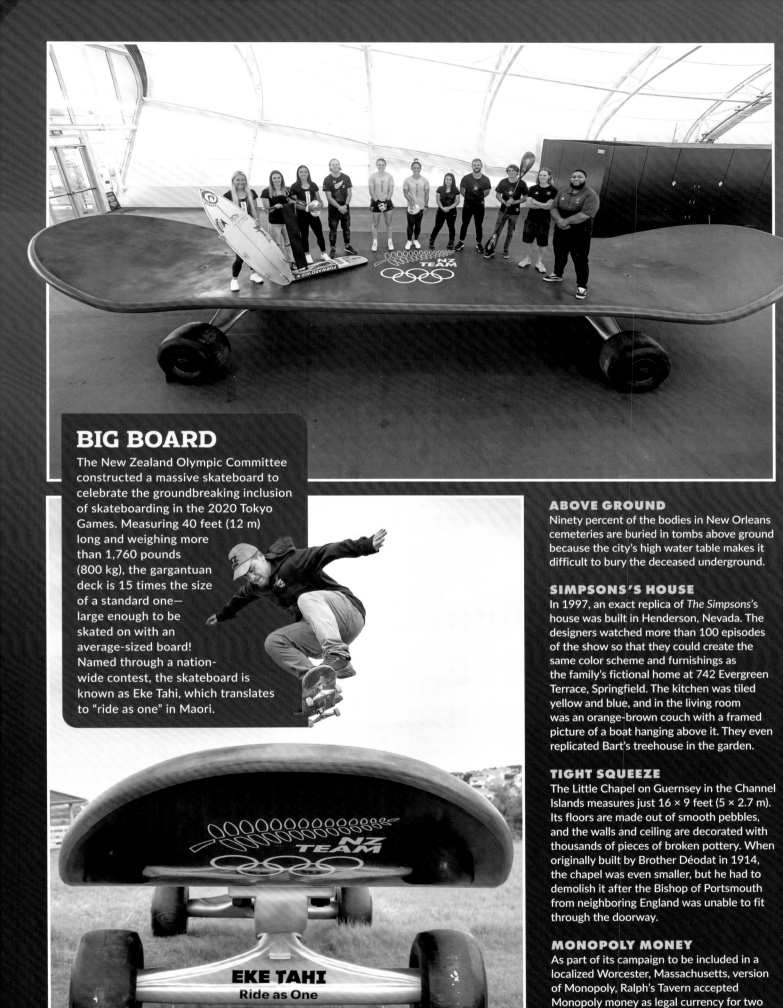

BIG BOARD

The New Zealand Olympic Committee constructed a massive skateboard to celebrate the groundbreaking inclusion of skateboarding in the 2020 Tokyo Games. Measuring 40 feet (12 m) long and weighing more than 1,760 pounds (800 kg), the gargantuan deck is 15 times the size of a standard one—large enough to be skated on with an average-sized board! Named through a nation-wide contest, the skateboard is known as Eke Tahi, which translates to "ride as one" in Maori.

EKE TAHI
Ride as One

ABOVE GROUND

Ninety percent of the bodies in New Orleans cemeteries are buried in tombs above ground because the city's high water table makes it difficult to bury the deceased underground.

SIMPSONS'S HOUSE

In 1997, an exact replica of *The Simpsons*'s house was built in Henderson, Nevada. The designers watched more than 100 episodes of the show so that they could create the same color scheme and furnishings as the family's fictional home at 742 Evergreen Terrace, Springfield. The kitchen was tiled yellow and blue, and in the living room was an orange-brown couch with a framed picture of a boat hanging above it. They even replicated Bart's treehouse in the garden.

TIGHT SQUEEZE

The Little Chapel on Guernsey in the Channel Islands measures just 16 × 9 feet (5 × 2.7 m). Its floors are made out of smooth pebbles, and the walls and ceiling are decorated with thousands of pieces of broken pottery. When originally built by Brother Déodat in 1914, the chapel was even smaller, but he had to demolish it after the Bishop of Portsmouth from neighboring England was unable to fit through the doorway.

MONOPOLY MONEY

As part of its campaign to be included in a localized Worcester, Massachusetts, version of Monopoly, Ralph's Tavern accepted Monopoly money as legal currency for two hours on June 23, 2021.

THE NANTUCKET *SEA SERPENT*

During the summer of 1937, a strange occurrence took Nantucket, Massachusetts, by storm as stories emerged of a mysterious sea serpent spotted in the waters surrounding the island, and locals scrambled to the beach for a one-of-a-kind reveal.

Within days, multiple witnesses came forward with tales of a creature unknown to science. They included local fisherman Bill Manville, who swore he'd witnessed an unknown creature gliding through the Atlantic waters off the coast. A fisherman named Gilbert Manter later confirmed Bill's story, claiming he'd also seen a strange marine animal while out angling for bluefish. Days later, Gilbert and his friend Ed Crocker stumbled across bizarre footprints on a beach near the recent sea-serpent sightings.

The tracks measured a massive 4 feet (1.2 m) wide by 5.5 feet (1.7 m) long.

Locals wondered if a previously unaccounted-for creature now haunted the waters and beaches of their quaint New England island. They received a definitive answer in July, when a massive monster washed ashore on South Beach (modern-day Francis Street Beach).

To the wonder of islanders and visitors, the strange creature had all of the trappings of a mythological sea serpent: dangerous-looking teeth, a forked tongue, horns, and a spiky dorsal fin. But instead of bone and flesh, the creature was crafted from canvas and rubber. An enormous, whimsical balloon, the Nantucket Sea Serpent proved to be the handiwork of famed puppeteer and illustrator Anthony "Tony" Frederick Sarg.

The so-called sea serpent was Tony's gift to Nantucket, which he often visited. Tony crafted the fantastic beast to draw visitors to the small island. The hoax required many months of planning and enlisted the help of locals, including Bill, Gilbert, and Ed. The result was a delightful diversion for island-goers and a story that would continue to be shared decades later.

The sea serpent later traveled to New York City, where it floated above the Macy's Thanksgiving Day Parade in 1937.

RARE PAIR

A twosome of turtles in Barnstable, Massachusetts, hatched from the same egg sharing a shell, six legs, and two heads!

The conjoined hatchlings are diamond terrapin turtles and were named Mary-Kate and Ashley after the famous Olsen twins. Their condition, known as bicephaly, is a rare anomaly triggered by environmental or genetic factors. In the wild, they wouldn't stand a chance of survival. Fortunately, the tiny duo hatched from a protected nesting site, were soon spotted, and found their way to the Birdsey Cape Wildlife Center, where they've received expert care.

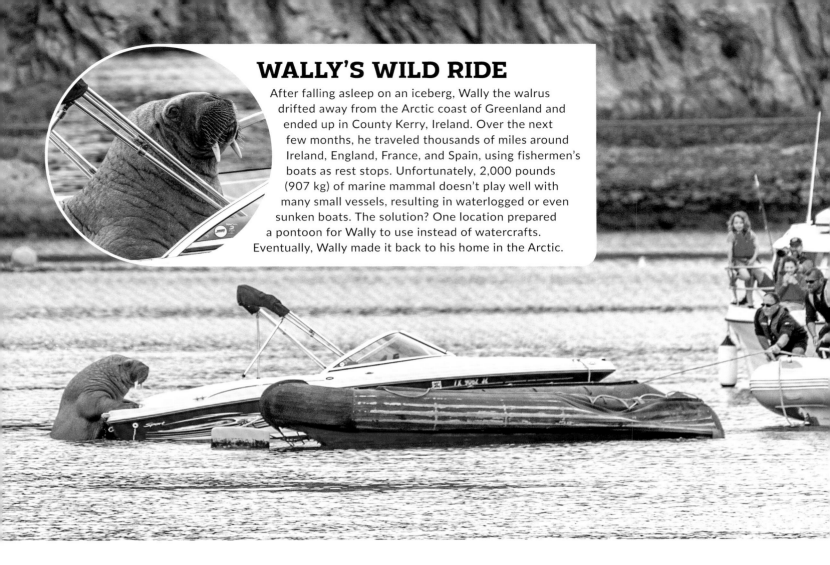

WALLY'S WILD RIDE

After falling asleep on an iceberg, Wally the walrus drifted away from the Arctic coast of Greenland and ended up in County Kerry, Ireland. Over the next few months, he traveled thousands of miles around Ireland, England, France, and Spain, using fishermen's boats as rest stops. Unfortunately, 2,000 pounds (907 kg) of marine mammal doesn't play well with many small vessels, resulting in waterlogged or even sunken boats. The solution? One location prepared a pontoon for Wally to use instead of watercrafts. Eventually, Wally made it back to his home in the Arctic.

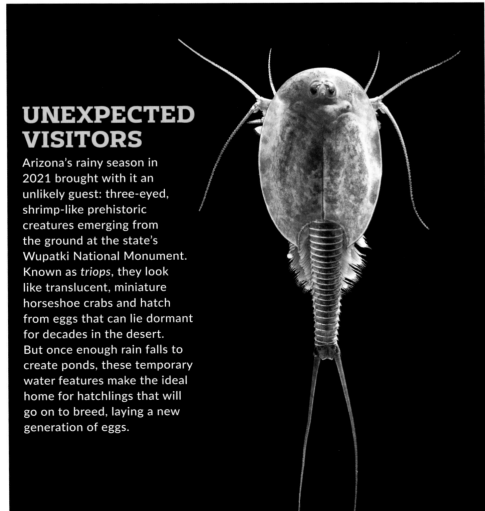

UNEXPECTED VISITORS

Arizona's rainy season in 2021 brought with it an unlikely guest: three-eyed, shrimp-like prehistoric creatures emerging from the ground at the state's Wupatki National Monument. Known as *triops*, they look like translucent, miniature horseshoe crabs and hatch from eggs that can lie dormant for decades in the desert. But once enough rain falls to create ponds, these temporary water features make the ideal home for hatchlings that will go on to breed, laying a new generation of eggs.

MINIATURE MOTORBIKES

Chuai Mege, a former automobile mechanic from Jilin City, China, carves amazingly detailed miniature motorcycles out of wood. Each one can take him a whole year to complete because he often needs to carve more than 700 separate parts, including tires, the dashboard, and even individual screws.

INDOOR CLIMB

John Griffin climbed the 30 stairs of his three-story house in Shoreham, England, 1,363 times in 29 hours. His total of 40,890 steps represented a vertical climb of 29,037 feet (8,853 m)—the height of Mount Everest. As he also had to walk back down the stairs each time, he reached the bottom of Everest only a few seconds after reaching the top!

NOT EXTINCT

When a black-browed babbler bird was found living in Borneo in 2020, it was the first sighting of the species anywhere in the world for over 170 years.

FATAL FARTS

Beaded lacewing larvae immobilize their prey with toxic flatulence. The insect larva feeds on termites, and when hungry, it releases a potent vapor from its anus that can stun up to six termites at a time.

ECLECTIC ELECTRIC

For more than 50 years, the Consumer Electronics Expo (CES) has provided a global stage to showcase some of the world's most outlandish innovations.

The yearly convention highlights wacky gadgets, weird inventions, and tech solutions to problems you don't even know you have (yet)! While it may be a while before these products are in stores, here are some of the most bizarre devices to appear at CES in recent years.

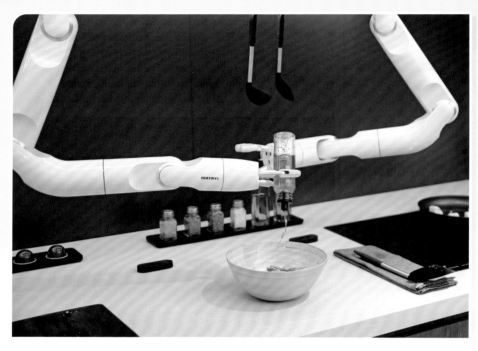

BOT CHEF

Samsung's Bot Chef looks like a kitchen cabinet that's sprouted arms. The "arms" rely on computer vision algorithms and artificial intelligence to identify ingredients and equipment—including knives. But don't worry about the robot uprising just yet; Bot Chef is programmed to stop moving when humans come near.

WELLNESS TOILET

Wonder what's up down under? Give the Toto Wellness Toilet a whirl. While it may sound gross, what you leave in the commode holds a wealth of health information. The Wellness Toilet analyzes fecal matter and urine with every flush, and also provides health recommendations via a phone app.

ROLLBOT

Never get stranded on the porcelain throne without paper with Charmin's RollBot. This ingenious AI offers a lifeline in a paperless pinch. Just use your cell phone (because who goes to the bathroom without one these days?) to initiate the Bluetooth-enabled toilet paper delivery sidekick.

BREADBOT

Wilkinson Baking Company's BreadBot churns out piping hot loaves of bread every six minutes. The state-of-the-art vending machine handles mixing, kneading, proofing, and baking. It adjusts ingredients based on atmospheric conditions, and a tablet aids customers in selecting the freshest loaves.

QOOBO

Many therapeutic benefits accompany owning a pet, but for those unable or unwilling to care for animals, there's Qoobo. This furry cushion/robot reacts to sounds with "lifelike" tail motions, inviting users to stroke and hold it. First appearing at CES 2018, a variety of colors and sizes are now available to adopt.

GAMER GUM

Serious gamers require quick energy without coffee-making, snacking, or other independent use of their hands—hence, XPG Mana Gaming Chewing Gum. This mint-flavored pick-me-up includes ingredients you need, like caffeine and lutein (for eye health), without ones you don't (like sugar).

FOLDIMATE

The Foldimate effortlessly transforms heaps of clean laundry into drawer-worthy items. Just feed clothing into the machine, and it'll spit out a ready-to-put-away pile seconds later. Foldimate's creators claim it takes just five minutes for it to fold a hamper-full.

As a player with NBA team Oklahoma City Thunder, Russell Westbrook always started layup drills with his teammates when the pregame clock showed exactly 6:17.

WORLD TOUR
After Christian Gogos's children and their friends wrote a message in a bottle and tossed it into the River Rhine in Bonn, Germany, it washed up seven years later on the other side of the world on a beach in Auckland, New Zealand—around 11,300 miles (18,185 km) away.

VOLCANO HIGHWIRE
On March 4, 2020, in foggy conditions, Nik Wallenda walked a 1,800-foot-long (549-m) steel highwire suspended above the active lava lake of the Masaya Volcano in Nicaragua. Even though he wore a gas mask and goggles, the toxic sulfur dioxide gases emanating from the lava filled the air with a stench of rotten eggs and burned his eyes.

TRANSPARENT SQUID
The rare googly-eyed glass squid, which lives in the depths of the southern oceans, has a transparent body, and when threatened it fills itself with water to appear bigger and more intimidating. If that tactic fails, it releases ink and uses jet propulsion to escape.

BASEBALL MASKS
During the Spanish flu epidemic, a baseball game was staged in Pasadena, California, where everyone wore protective face coverings. When the Pasadena Merchants played the Standard-Murphys in a game in the Southern California Winter League on January 26, 1919, the players, umpires, spectators, and even the mascot's dog all wore linen and cheesecloth face masks.

WORM WONDER
Four out of every five animals on Earth is a nematode worm. There are 57 billion nematodes for every human.

SCORPION VENOM
The most expensive liquid in the world is the venom of the deathstalker scorpion, native to North Africa and the Middle East. Its venom, which is 100 times more painful than a bee sting, sells for up to $39 million a gallon!

OUTHOUSE ATTACK
While using an outhouse in the backcountry near Haines, Alaska, Shannon Stevens was bitten from below by a bear. As soon as she sat on the toilet, she felt something bite her. Her brother Erik heard her scream and went to investigate, and when he raised the toilet seat, he came face-to-face with the bear! He quickly shut the lid and ran.

LONG WAIT
In 2021, Mandy Prior was finally reunited with her cat Taz—14 years after he escaped through an open bathroom window at their home in Dorset, England. She spotted him on a lost-and-found pets page on Facebook.

TONS OF TOMATOES
Douglas Smith of Stanstead Abbotts, Hertfordshire, England, grew a staggering 1,269 tomatoes on a single stem! Astonishingly enough, this was not long after he had cultivated 839 tomatoes on one stem. Both of these, however, break the previous known record of 488 by a long shot! What's Douglas's secret? Choosing the right variety, to begin with, plus dedicating several hours a week making sure the tomato plant has enough water, nutrients, sunlight, and support.

STAR POWER

REACH FOR THE STAR!

During Italy's Sa Sartiglia Festival in Oristano, horseback riders wearing eerie blank-faced doll masks gallop through the city's crowded streets in hot pursuit of a star-shaped token.

Up to 120 knights participate in the thrilling race, and it culminates with one equestrian skewering the tin star with their sword or spear. But the adrenaline-packed spectacle doesn't stop there. Other so-called "knights" take part in stunning acrobatic horseback displays divided into three teams. Medieval manuscripts date the festival to at least the fourteenth century, although some speculate the event is much older.

ONE HUNDRED AND FOURTEEN

The Pequod Meets The Bachelor

And jolly enough were the sights and the sounds that came bearing down before the wind, some few week after Ahab's harpoon had been welded.

It was a Nantucket ship, the Bachelor, which had just wedged in her last cask of oil, and bolted down her bursting hatches; and now, in glad holiday apparel was joyously, though somewhat vain-gloriously, sailing round among the widely-seperated ships on the ground, previous to pointing her prow for home.

MOBY DICK

by

Herman Melville

Ripley's Exhibit
Cat. No. 170522

MOBY DICK ON TOILET PAPER

The entire text of the 1851 novel *Moby Dick* typed onto toilet paper typed by Dennis Malone of Palm Springs, Florida. The book contains more than 200,000 words, and it took six rolls to cover the whole novel.

Ripley's Exhibit
Cat. No. 171301

GARLIC PAINTING

Detailed painting titled *Harvesting* created with layers of garlic oil by artist Mark Lawrence Libunao of Manila in the Philippines. In order to preserve his work, Mark created an organic preservative that gives his art a shelf life of 50 years.

Corner view.

EMULSIFIER

Exactly 160 glass pieces individually painted and arranged in a cube to create a different image when viewed from every side—a fish, a bird, a clockwork fish, and a bird skeleton. Created by artist Thomas Medicus of Innsbruck, Austria.

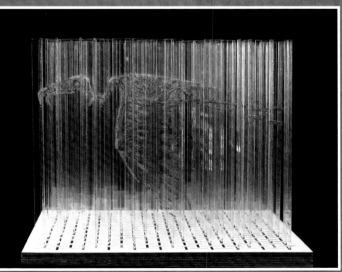

INVASIVE SPECIES

About 100 elephants roamed London in the summer of 2021, and although these sculptures didn't live and breathe, they helped raise awareness about the effect humans can have on wild spaces.

The life-size masterpieces stand up to 15 feet (4.6 m) tall and can weigh about 800 pounds (363 kg) each. The figures are crafted out of *Lantana camara*, a highly invasive weed harmful to native habitats, which has spread worldwide after being brought to Europe by explorers. The environmental art campaign is a collaboration between nonprofits The Real Elephant Collective and Elephant Family, and it showed up in places like London's Royal Parks and Berkeley Square, with plans to go worldwide.

AFTER

BEFORE

WOOLLY THICK

After spending about seven years in the wild, a sheep named Baarack had grown a wool coat weighing 78 pounds (35.4 kg)! Domestic sheep will grow their wool indefinitely and need to be sheared on a regular basis. Baarack was carrying nearly half his weight in wool and struggled to survive as the burden it made it difficult for him to see, forage, or even walk. But shearing has transformed this four-legged friend into a recognizable—and incredibly lightweight—sheep who can happily graze and move about once more.

DRINKING AND FLYING

Swifts spend nearly their entire lives flying and will drink by skimming water off the surface of lakes and other bodies of water without breaking flight. Believe it or not, it's actually easier for them to drink this way because their short legs and long wings make it awkward for them to perch. These birds will even sleep and mate mid-air, too. The only things that brings them to the ground? Making nests, laying eggs, and raising young.

GRACE GOOD

World-renowned circus artist Grace Good astonishes audiences with aerial feats and fiery stunts, as well as impressive hoop and balancing acts— sometimes combining them all into one jaw-dropping spectacle!

Grace began her circus journey teaching herself hoop tricks as a hobby in college, but she soon grew to love the art and began adding extra hoops and fire. Determined to make a career out of hooping, she left school and began performing on the streets of Nashville, Tennessee. There she was approached by a circus aerialist, who took Grace under her wings. What followed was a whirlwind adventure of learning other circus acts, joining a touring company, going viral on social media, and performing on national television.

Grace has earned great success, but that doesn't mean she has stopped pushing herself. One of her most recent tricks and biggest challenges to date involves her hanging from an aerial silk by one hand while keeping multiple hoops spinning around her body! Believe it or not, Grace begins the feat while balanced atop her iconic "big red ball," which is almost as tall as she is!

STAYING AFLOAT

For the foodie on the cutting edge of culinary trends, there's a riverside restaurant near Bangkok, Thailand, where guests eat amid calf-deep floodwater.

Owner Titiporn Jutimanon stumbled upon the idea when the rising tide of the Chao Phraya River threatened to close his restaurant, Chaopraya Antique Café. Instead of shutting down, he decided to stay open and turn the flooding into an experience. What Titiporn did in desperation proved to be a stroke of genius as people started flocking to his eatery to dine among the waves. Customers get an added splash whenever boats cruise by, sending water barreling into the dining area.

COTTON CASTLE

Turkey's most popular attraction, Pamukkale, translates to "Cotton Castle." And there's no better name for this strange natural landscape. Visitors to the mystical place will find layers of white stone formed by mineral pools and filled with water that has purported health benefits. And right next door are the well-preserved ruins of the Greco-Roman metropolis Hierapolis. This mystical and historic destination draws two million visitors each year.

ANIMAL AMMUNITION
During medieval sieges, soldiers would often load a trebuchet (a giant catapult) with the carcass of a dead animal and fire it into enemy territory in the hope that it would spread disease behind the castle's walls.

SHORTS VOW
On November 24, 2019, Winnipeg Blue Bombers fan Chris Matthew wore pants instead of shorts for the first time in 18 years after his favorite football team finally won the Grey Cup. In 2001, he had vowed to wear shorts every day—even in snow—until the Bombers won the cup.

DOG PATROL
Every day during the summer of 2020, a stray dog named Kursha showed up at a pedestrian crossing in Batumi in the country of Georgia to help a kindergarten class safely cross the road. Patrolling up and down as the children crossed, the dog stood in front of vehicles and barked if any tried to edge forward. It only stepped out of the way when the last child had gone.

INTERNET DISTRACTION
The city government in Bandung, Indonesia, gave out pet chicks to 2,000 elementary and middle school students in the hope that caring for the birds would keep the children off the internet and their smartphones.

UNDERWATER TORNADO
Schmidt Ocean Institute researchers discovered a mysterious underwater tornado on the ocean floor off the coast of Queensland, Australia. No one knows what caused the swirling tornado, which left a short trail in its wake and was similar to dust devils found on land.

FAST FOOD
The atmosphere on Venus is so hot you could cook a 16-inch pizza in under 10 seconds just by holding it out to the air.

COD KISSING
Visitors to Newfoundland, Canada, can take part in a welcome ceremony known as a "screech-in" where they kiss the mouth of a dead cod before drinking a shot of rum known as a screech. In some instances, participants are also required to eat a piece of "Newfoundland steak"—a.k.a. baloney.

SUPERHERO STORE
As well as costumes, masks, and capes, the Brooklyn Superhero Supply Company store in New York City sells a range of superpowers, including half-pint cans of omnipotence and immortality, gallon bottles of antigravity, and jars of invisibility. Like all good crime-fighters, the store itself has a secret identity, operating as a front for a learning center for young students interested in creative writing.

BITE-SIZED
These pearl-sized, frost-resistant apples were grown to thrive in Yakutsk, Russia, where the average winter temperature sits at a chilly -29°F (-34°C). Cultivated by Nikifor Ivanov, these miniature fruits endure frigid temperatures, yet still have a crunchy, appley flavor. The diminished size of the plants represents an adaptation to the extreme environment. But Nikifor reports that harvesting the marble-sized produce is quite a chore and much of the fruit gets eaten as it is picked.

TINY BUT MIGHTY

Some of nature's deadliest creatures come in deceptively small packages, but don't let their size fool you.

What they lack in size, they make up for in powerful poison or venom. What's the difference? Poison must be ingested, such as through eating, or absorbed through skin to be effective. Venomous animals, however, actively inject their toxins by biting or stinging. Make no mistake, you don't want to tangle with one of these teeny-tiny creatures, as some unlucky folks have found out the hard way.

BULLDOG ANTS

Ninety species of bulldog ants live in Australia, and they prove genuinely terrifying. Their pincers make up a terrifying amount of their small, 1.5-inch-long (3.8-cm) bodies. Known for aggressively jumping at intruders, they inflict a powerful sting that has killed at least three humans.

ASSASSIN CATERPILLARS

South America's assassin caterpillar lives up to its dangerous reputation. Covered in toxic brown spines, these hairy projectiles deliver a dangerous venom known to cause death in humans. Yet, the blood-thinning properties of the toxin may also have medicinal applications still being studied.

CONE SNAILS

There are hundreds of species of cone snails living on the planet, chiefly in tropical areas, but only a handful are lethal to humans. They hunt using a barbed dart, which they strike into their victims like a harpoon. The smallest cone snails deliver enough venom to rival a bee sting. But larger ones (about the size of your thumb) release a boatload of toxins capable of killing an adult within a few hours.

POISON DART FROGS

Poison dart frogs come in a rainbow of vibrant hues, but don't let their pretty packages mislead you. Those colors are animal-talk for "Stay away!" These small amphibians may look unassuming, but they hide a secret weapon. The golden dart frog, for example, is coated with enough poison to kill several humans in just minutes.

INDIAN RED SCORPIONS

The Indian red scorpion is considered by some to be the most lethal scorpion in the world. This brownish-red predatory arachnid has telltale dark gray ridges. It stings in defense, inflicting a deadly wound. Measuring up to just 3.5 inches (8.9 cm) long, it has small claws and a thick tail with a bulbous stinger.

FLAMBOYANT CUTTLEFISH

Off the Indo-Pacific waters of New Guinea and Australia lives an eye-popping beauty, the 3-inch-long (7.6-cm) flamboyant cuttlefish. Dark brown with purple and yellow pops of color, its changing patterns have a hypnotic effect on prey. These vibrant colors also bear witness to a dangerous secret: When eaten, it proves just as toxic as the infamous blue-ringed octopus.

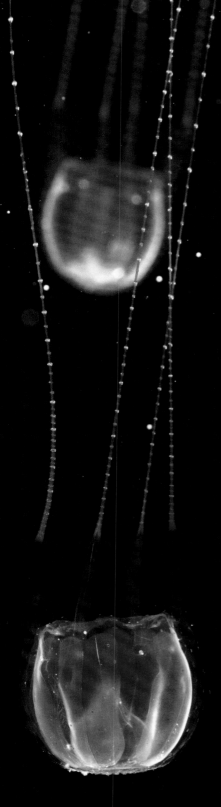

IRUKANDJI JELLIES

Each year, Irukandji jellies send between 50 to 100 people to the hospital. Translucent and measuring less than 0.5 inches (1.3 cm), they hang out in the coastal waters of northern Australia. Their venom causes a lethal condition called Irukandji syndrome, known to impart an impending sense of doom and cause many other painful symptoms, such as fatal brain hemorrhages.

WHIP IT GOOD

If a whip and a sword could have a love child, it would be the *urumi*. Essential to the martial art of Kalaripayattu, the *urumi* hasn't been actively used in warfare for generations. Part of the reason might have to do with its hazardous nature. After all, it can take many years to master—especially the multi-bladed versions. Nevertheless, the skill set is both deadly and graceful, drawing elements from performative dance and yoga.

GOALBALL

Invented in 1946, the sport of goalball requires players to cover their eyes and rely solely on touch and sound!

Goalball has been included in the Paralympic Games since its debut in Toronto, Canada, in 1976. Designed for those with visual impairments, the game involves throwing a 2.76-pound (1.25-kg) ball across a court to score, as well as defending against shots from the opposing team. Blocking involves players' entire bodies, thrown to the floor as rapidly as possible. After all, balls have been measured leaving athletes' hands at more than 37 mph (60 kmph)! The eyeshades ensure a level playing field among players with varying degrees of sight loss. To guide the athletes, the ball is fitted with bells and the court has raised lines.

HEADS UP

A 65.6-foot-tall (20-m) black-and-white head floating over Tokyo in summer 2021 might have left some citizens unsure if they were awake or dreaming. The strange sight was part of the Tokyo Tokyo Festival, an arts and culture celebration that coincided with the Olympic Games (which were also held in the city in 2021). Titled *Masayume*, or "prophetic dream," the hot-air balloon was created by the artist group known as "Me" and features the face of a real person who was chosen from more than a thousand applicants.

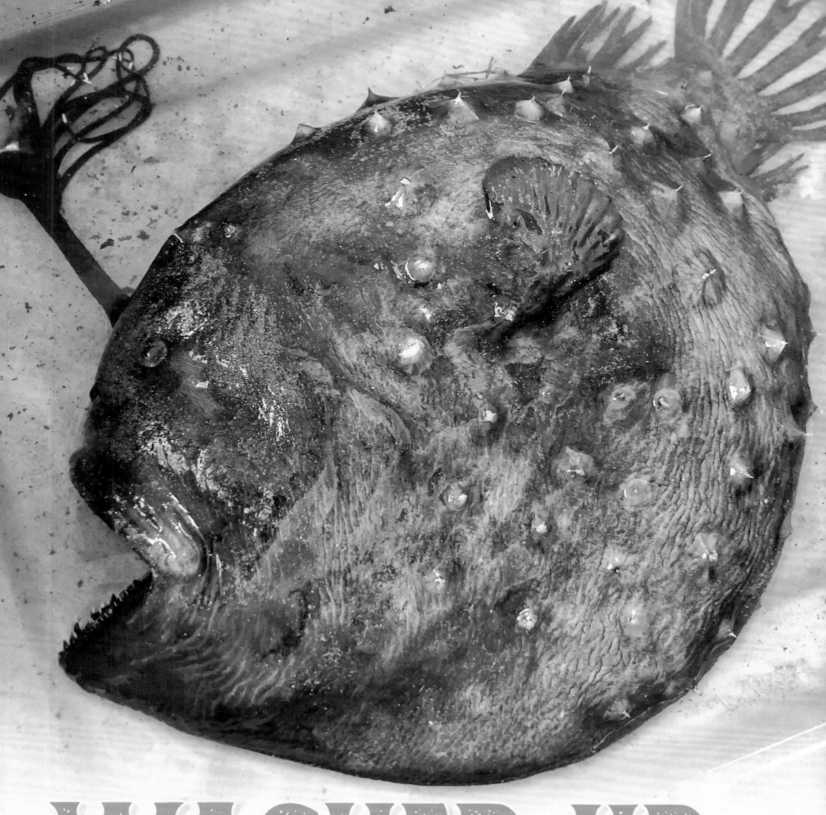

WASHED UP

A beachcomber visiting Crystal Cove State Park in Newport Beach, California, in May 2021 stumbled across a one-of-a-kind find: a Pacific footballfish that washed ashore.

What makes this such a rare find? A species of anglerfish, Pacific footballfish live between 2,000 and 3,300 feet (610 to 1,006 m) below the water's surface. They rely on overhead lamp-like lures that attract prey toward their toothy mouths using a phosphorescent light. Even more surprising, the 18-inch (46-cm) carcass appeared well-preserved and intact, despite its inexplicable journey to a beach in the Golden State.

SEA PEN

A fluffy sea pen may resemble an old-fashioned quill, but don't let this ocean floor creature's appearance fool you! Neither a writing device nor a plant, the sea pen is a collection of many tiny individual lifeforms, similar to anemones. A bulb anchors the sea pen to the ocean floor, and a primary polyp forms the stalk of the sea pen after losing its tentacles. From there, secondary polyps make the feathery branchlike structure of the quill, creating a cooperative colony. Believe it or not, some species glow when disturbed!

SPLASH OF COLOR

Garfish live in the open ocean and can swim with astonishing speed because of their slender, snake-like bodies, but it's their blue-green bones that make most people do a double-take. Their bones' electric color deters most people from eating them, although they are quite edible. People often jump to conclusions based on the color of their bones, assuming the bright hue is the result of radiation or decay. However, the actual cause of the strange color is a natural pigment called biliverdin.

EVEN THEIR TEETH ARE GREEN!

THE PEEL P50

The Peel P50 is the world's smallest production car, standing just 54 inches (137 cm) tall!

When it was first manufactured in 1962, the P50 was marketed as a commuter car capable of seating "one adult and a shopping bag" and sold for just £199 ($270 USD). The car had no reverse gear, just a handle on the back that allowed the driver to lift the car onto its front wheels and move the 130-pound (59-kg) vehicle around.

About 50 Peel P50s were made in the early '60s, with fewer than 30 originals still existing today. Those original models sell for big bucks these days, with one going for $140,250 at auction in 2017. Luckily, for those wanting to travel tiny, Peel Engineering began producing cars again in 2011.

The new P50s come in multiple versions, including an eco-friendly electric model, and are much more affordable compared to vintage originals. Want the Peel experience but aren't ready to commit to a new car? You can hop behind the wheel virtually in the *Forza Horizon* Xbox game series, instead!

Peel also manufactures the Trident, a two-seater car with a clear dome roof.

Peel cars can be found at Ripley's Believe It or Not! Odditoriums around the world. Visit a location near you and see how you measure up!

PEELIN' OUT

To raise money for the BBC Children in Need charity, Alex Orchin of Wivelsfield, England, drove the entire length of Great Britain in a Peel P50!

He set off on November 13, 2021, from John o'Groats, Scotland—the northernmost part of mainland Great Britain. The journey was not an easy one. Along the way, Alex battled freezing snow, hazardous road conditions, and various car troubles. But he wasn't alone. To keep him company was his friend Joely Raffel, who followed Alex in a camper van. The 874-mile (1,407-km) adventure concluded on December 4, 2021, when they reached the southernmost point of Great Britain—Land's End, England. Overall, they raised more than £11,000 ($14,900 USD) for Children in Need.

PEEL P50 STATS

130 POUNDS (59 KG)

28 MPH (45 KMPH) TOP SPEED

1 DOOR

1 HEADLIGHT

54 INCHES (137 CM) TALL

3 TIRES, 13 INCHES (34.2 CM) TALL

BRITAIN'S BIGGEST JOURNEY IN THE WORLD'S SMALLEST CAR!

REMARKABLE REPLICA

Nothing's as creepy and kooky, mysterious and spooky as this *Addams Family* dollhouse created by miniature artist Kelly Little-Kuehnert of Knightstown, Indiana.

The house took more than one year and "too many hours to count" to craft, according to Kelly. Commissioned by Linda LaPage, it features dolls by Lillian Bass and a spooktacular family car by Vanessa Busti. What's most remarkable about the dollhouse is the incredible attention to detail, from the taxidermy-stuffed living room where Lurch dusts to the dining room with its own miniature version of the *Addams Family* house. Gomez and Morticia's bedroom has real silk sheets, Wednesday plays with her favorite electric chair "toy," and the entryway holds family photos and the infamous polar bear rug, Bruno.

A coral reef discovered in 2020 at the northern tip of Australia's Great Barrier Reef stands 1,640 feet (500 m) high, making it taller than the Empire State Building.

REAL BATMOBILE
Nguyen Dac Chung, an architecture student from Hanoi, Vietnam, spent over $20,000 building his own functional Batmobile as it appeared in the 2008 film *The Dark Knight*. The Batman-inspired vehicle is powered by a four-cylinder, 400cc engine and has a top speed of 62 mph (100 kmph).

YOUNG KAYAKER
At age 10, Bodie Hilleke, of Glenwood Springs, Colorado, kayaked all 280 miles (450 km) of the Colorado River through the Grand Canyon. Bodie, who started kayaking when he was five, took 18 days to complete the epic journey.

JIGSAW PUZZLE
Maxine Olive, of Belleville, Ontario, Canada, completed a 40,320-piece jigsaw puzzle in 150 hours. She worked up to 16 hours a day for nine days straight on the giant puzzle, which depicts popular Disney characters. It measures 22 × 6 feet (6.7 × 1.8 m) and took up her entire living room.

NOSE GUARDS
Bottlenose dolphins often use sea sponges to protect their sensitive beaks while foraging for fish on the rocky ocean floor. Before going off hunting, they will tear a marine basket sponge from the ocean floor and wear it over the tip of their beak.

FREE FLIGHTS
In October 2020, Frontier Airlines offered free flights to Orlando, Florida, for anyone with the first or last name Orlando.

EDIBLE PAINT
Sally Magdy Murad, a young Egyptian artist, creates detailed portraits of famous Arab personalities using ingredients such as honey, chocolate, syrup, candy, raisins, and molasses as her paints. She applies these foodstuffs to the canvas with spoons and toothpicks instead of brushes.

KARAOKE MARATHON
In August 2020, Jacqueline Brits and Rhinus Lotz, of Mbombela, South Africa, sang karaoke for 35 hours straight at a local bar.

SOLO CANAL
Using only basic hand tools, Laungi Bhuiyan spent more than 30 years single-handedly digging a 1.9-mile-long (3-km) canal to his home village of Kothilawa, India. His 4-foot-wide (1.2-m), 3-foot-deep (0.9-m) canal brings much-needed rainwater from surrounding hills to a pond near the village.

SEA FOOD

Scuba diving enthusiast Sergio Gamberini has combined his passions for gardening and exploring the ocean through underwater growing domes for land-based plants.

Sergio planted his first under-ocean vegetable plot, Nemo's Garden, off the coast of Noli, Italy, in 2012. He started by growing basil in an experimental biosphere and enjoyed great success. Since that time, Sergio has upped his game and now cultivates more than 100 types of plants under the sea, including strawberries, flowers, and tomatoes. Remarkably, the plants flourish despite growing more than 20 feet (6 m) beneath the Mediterranean Sea, thanks in part to the high humidity and increased pressure.

ROOFTOP GARDEN

Hit hard by the 2020 pandemic, the Ratchapruk and Bovorn Taxi companies of Bangkok, Thailand, were left with more than 2,500 taxi cabs parked for months. To make use of the roof space atop the idle vehicles, they encouraged drivers to plant community gardens there. Each "plot" is situated atop black plastic garbage bags stretched across bamboo frames, and plants include cucumbers, tomatoes, and string beans.

WILD HAIR

When it comes to bizarre hairdos, human beings have nothing on the animal kingdom.

Some animals rely on outlandish appearances to help attract mates, and others use eclectic fur-scapes for camouflage. Meanwhile, domesticated creatures like dogs and livestock can thank human breeders for their specialized looks. Here's our breakdown of some of nature's most eye-catching coiffed creatures.

ROCKHOPPER PENGUIN

Rockhopper penguins live in colonies on the Falkland Islands and Tristan da Cunha near Antarctica. Unlike other penguin species who've perfected "dapper" with their black-and-white tuxedo appearances, rockhoppers prefer a punk-rock vibe. A crest of long golden feathers crowns their head like an array of spikes gelled into place.

THISTLEDOWN VELVET ANT

Despite its name, the thistledown velvet ant is really a parasitic wasp. It was long thought that the flightless female's wispy white hairs were a way to hide amongst the fluffy fruits of the creosote bush. But new research suggests their Einstein-like appearance helps keep them cool in the deserts of the western U.S. and Mexico, where they have lived long before the creosote bush ever arrived!

MANGALITSA PIG

It's no wonder why Mangalitsa pigs are also known as "sheep pigs." The breed originated in Hungary, where its thick, woolly coat keeps it warm in near-freezing winter temperatures. Unfortunately for the Mangalitsa pigs, the phrase "cute enough to eat" rings all too true, as they are highly prized for their fatty, flavorful meat.

VICTORIA CROWNED PIGEON

Victoria crowned pigeons are among the largest of all pigeons, nearly rivaling turkeys in size. They boast stunning deep blue coloring with scarlet contrasts. But it's the prominent feather crests atop their heads, resembling wispy, whimsical crowns, that make these natives of Papua New Guinea and Indonesia so recognizable.

MARY RIVER TURTLE

Australia's Mary River turtle is one of the biggest nonconformists of the animal kingdom thanks to its emerald-colored "hair," which is actually algae! The turtle can breathe through its cloaca (its opening for peeing, pooping, and reproduction), allowing the reptile to spend up to three days underwater at a time and giving the green toupee plenty of time to take root.

COTTON-TOP TAMARIN

Colombia's cotton-top tamarin wears a shock of white fluff on its head. The style resembles a combination between a mullet and a mohawk, with the hair appearing longer in the back and nonexistent on the sides of the primate's head. The bushy white fur is also on its chest and underbelly, with its back covered in dark brown hair.

BERGAMASCO SHEPHERD

Despite the Bergamasco shepherd's stunning array of locks, which create layers of flat, felted hair, it's a surprisingly low-maintenance dog. Yes, these distinctive pooches roll out of bed looking *this* good. But the style serves functional uses, too, protecting the canines from wild predators and frigid Alpine temperatures.

70 PERCENT

The percentage of the world's population—more than five billion people—who do not use toilet paper.

FAMILY LINK

Defying odds of one in 2.1 million, a baby girl was born on leap day just like her father. Ivan Rebollar Cortez was born on February 29, 1988, and daughter Camila entered the world on February 29, 2020, in Carmichael, California—just as her 32-year-old father was celebrating his eighth leap-day birthday.

RUDE AWAKENING

Before alarm clocks were invented, factories in the UK employed people known as knocker-uppers to tap on workers' bedroom windows with a long stick to make sure they were not late for work.

DESERT MYSTERY

In 1969, American musician Jim Sullivan recorded an album, *U.F.O.*, which featured lyrics about leaving his family and being abducted by aliens in the desert. Six years later, he vanished without trace in the New Mexico desert, leaving behind his abandoned car containing his money, clothes, and guitar.

VINTAGE WATCH

When a Canadian woman dropped her phone down her $25 thrift-store couch, she reached between the cushions to retrieve it and found a rare, vintage Rolex Daytona Paul Newman watch worth $250,000.

GETTING 'ROUND

Inventor Bernhard Sobotta has combined the best of bicycling and camping in his latest creation: the Cercle Bike. Despite its streamlined and minimalist appearance, the Cercle Bike includes a built-in chair, desk, and bed. The frame can even be converted into a tent for those times when you don't want to sleep directly under the stars. Best of all, it's a cinch to pack up the tent and get back on the road!

HOMEWORK FIRE

When lost in the mountains near Whitewater Ski Resort in British Columbia, Canada, two 16-year-old snowboarders survived through the cold winter night by building a shelter and burning their school homework to stay warm.

BEATLES CONNECTION

Jim Carrey, who plays Dr. Ivo "Eggman" Robotnik in the 2020 movie *Sonic the Hedgehog*, covered the Beatles song "I Am the Walrus" for the band's former producer George Martin's 1998 album *In My Life*. That song contains the lyric "I am the eggman."

DANCING PENGUINS

All of the motion-capture performers for the 2006 movie *Happy Feet* first had to study the movements of penguins. For the dance sequences, they not only had to wear sensor suits but also special headgear to represent the penguins' beaks.

INSTANT SCULPTURES

Using only his bare hands and a clay sculpting knife, Yan Junhai, a street artist from Changsha, China, creates incredibly accurate clay busts of passersby in just a few minutes.

TRIBUTARY SANCTUARY

Floating along the Manatee River in Palmetto, Florida, is a houseboat unlike any other. Previously known as the "Chapel on the Bay," it was once the only floating, self-propelled wedding chapel in the United States. It contained 16 hand-carved pews and could accommodate up to 125 wedding guests. However, it turns out weddings on the water are not in high demand, so the chapel was sold and converted into a luxury houseboat in 2015. Not wanting to lose the property's charm, the new owners kept many of the chapel's iconic features, including the 30-foot (9-m) spire, stained glass windows, and arched wooden doors.

HOME SWEET HIVE

The residents of the village of Kandovan in northwest Iran have embraced life as modern cave-dwellers, living in homes hewn from rock and dating back roughly 700 years.

Located in the province of East Azerbaijan, the town's geological foundations come thanks to ash and debris deposited from the now-dormant Mount Sahand volcano, which blew its top 11,000 years ago. But people wouldn't get interested in burrowing into these structures until the Mongolian army invaded 10,300 years later. The threat of violent invasion from these nomadic warriors made hiding out in remote caves attractive. Although some have described the Kandovan village as looking like a giant termite colony, villagers prefer to call their homes "karan," which translates as "beehives" in the local Turkic dialect.

FRANKEN-*FAIRIES*

Netherlands-based artist Cedric Laquieze turns dead insects into fairies!

Cedric has created hundreds of these peculiar pixies since starting more than a decade ago, and no two are alike. To start, he carefully takes apart the ethically sourced insects' delicate exoskeletons and wings. Cedric can then rearrange and combine them into a new creation, sometimes using up to 10 insects in a single sculpture! By using a variety of colors, shapes, and textures, he can achieve different personalities, ranging from regal to whimsical. Cedric's other work includes flower-covered skeletons and anatomical models made from plastic toys.

ANATOMY OF A FRANKEN-*FAIRY*

BODY

TORSO

WINGS

UP TO 10 INSECTS IN A SINGLE SCULPTURE!

DESERTED KINGDOM

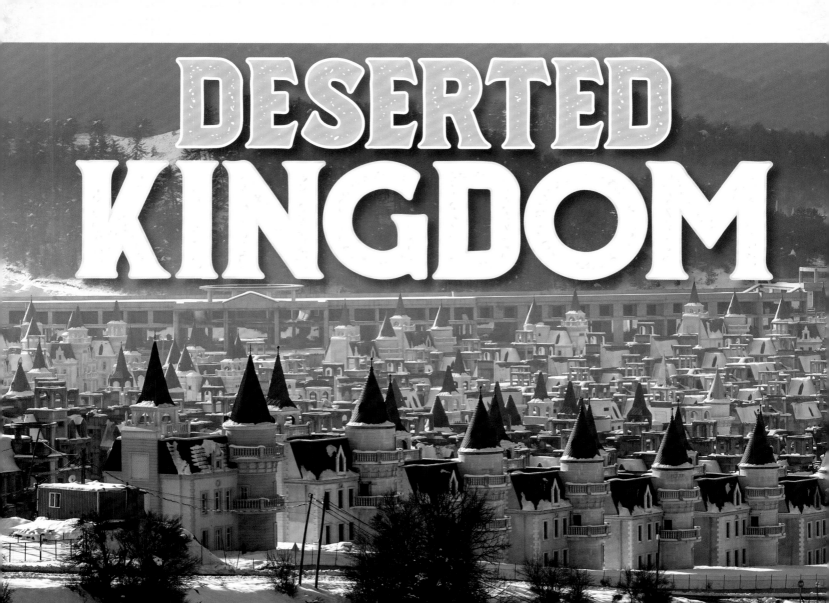

The world's most expensive ghost town is a sprawling housing development in northwestern Turkey populated by hundreds of identical castles.

Arranged in semicircles, the Burj Al Babas Villa looks more like a surreal M.C. Escher illustration than a high-end housing development. Surrounded by lush forests and rolling hills, the subdivision sits near the town of Mudurnu. The property developers behind the project had the ambitious goal of creating 732 luxurious, French-inspired châteaus. The company shelled out more than $200 million on the project, building 583 homes before construction came to a screeching halt due to economic woes.

FERTILIZER FEUD

Snowball fights are a winter staple in the Northern Hemisphere, and Spain is famed for its annual tomato-throwing festival, but you probably haven't heard of Gorehabba—a cow dung–hurling festival! It takes place among the villagers of Gumatapura, India. The manure is collected from nearby farms and brought to a temple where it is blessed before the battle begins. Hundreds of combatants participate in the fight, which brings the holiday of Diwali, or the festival of lights, to a close.

CULINARY CARVINGS

Franky Yeung Pui Kee of Toronto, Ontario, Canada, crafts extraordinary edible art from vegetables and fruit. A master of his craft, Franky uses a paring knife to turn produce into elaborate designs, from smiling Buddhas to ducks and even flashy, flying Chinese dragons. Drawing inspiration from an ancient art form centuries in the making, his take on this Chinese culinary tradition transforms radishes and carrots into awe-inspiring masterpieces.

Freddie Mercury used an upright piano as a headboard for his bed so that he could play tunes that came to him in his dreams.

TAPEWORM FLUSH

Kritsada Ratprachoom, from Udon Thani, Thailand, pulled a live, 32-foot-long (9.7-m) tapeworm out of his butt while he sat on the toilet. After the parasitic worm tried to wriggle out of the toilet bowl, he successfully flushed it away.

EARTH SANDWICH

Etienne Naude, from Auckland, New Zealand, and Angel Sierra, from southern Spain, created an Earth sandwich by placing slices of bread on the exact opposite sides of the world, 12,500 miles (20,000 km) apart, at the same time.

FIRST LAUGH

In Native American Navajo tradition, whenever a baby laughs for the first time the family throws a party, which is quickly organized by the person who made the baby laugh. The First Laugh Ceremony is usually held within a week of the first giggle.

LOOSE TOOTH

Ukrainian TV presenter Marichka Padalko caught her front tooth as it fell out live on air in 2020 while she was reading the news. She felt it come loose as she was speaking, so she put her hand in front of her mouth, caught it, and carried on without a pause.

CANNED CONDO

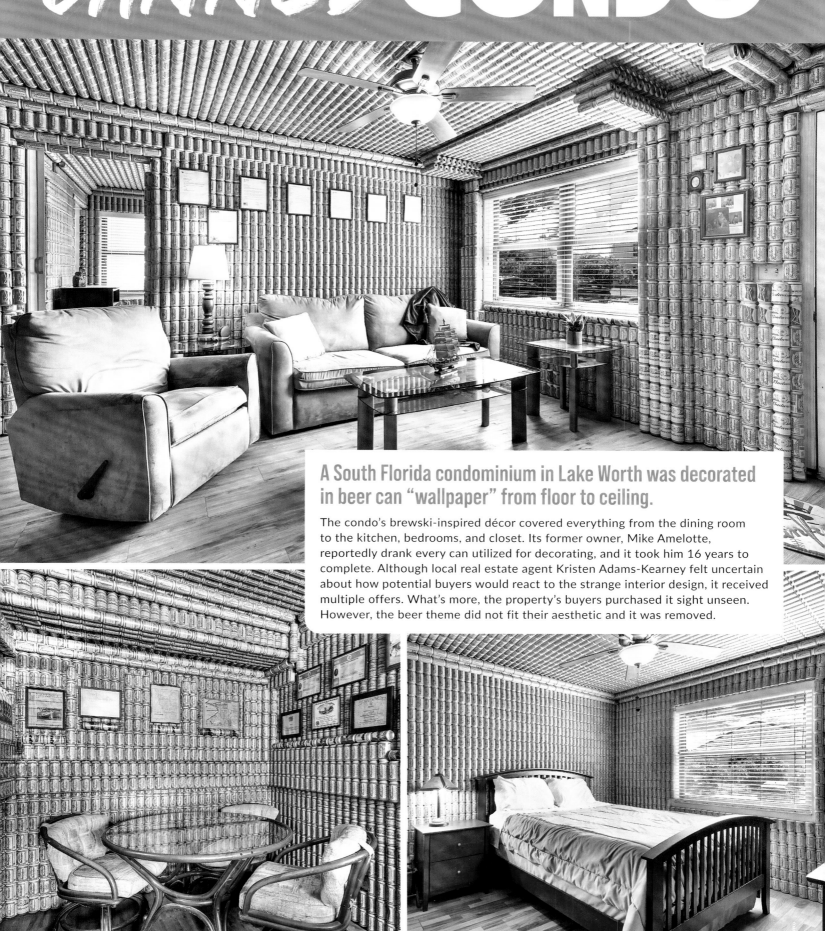

A South Florida condominium in Lake Worth was decorated in beer can "wallpaper" from floor to ceiling.

The condo's brewski-inspired décor covered everything from the dining room to the kitchen, bedrooms, and closet. Its former owner, Mike Amelotte, reportedly drank every can utilized for decorating, and it took him 16 years to complete. Although local real estate agent Kristen Adams-Kearney felt uncertain about how potential buyers would react to the strange interior design, it received multiple offers. What's more, the property's buyers purchased it sight unseen. However, the beer theme did not fit their aesthetic and it was removed.

Ripley's Exhibit
Cat. No. 23654

WHALE EAR BONE

Whales communicate through an amazing array of underwater whistles, clicks, and songs, and the way they hear is very different from animals living on land. Instead of sound traveling through ear canals like with land mammals, for toothed whales, it instead travels through their skin and into fatty sacks that lead to their large ear bones!

Ripley's Exhibit
Cat. No. 170664

MEGALODON TOOTH

Megalodon are an ancient, extinct species of shark—the largest that ever lived! Based on the size of their teeth, scientists estimate megalodon sharks reached about 65 feet (19.8 m) in length—longer than a bowling lane! Their teeth could grow up to 7 inches (17.8 cm) long! A great white shark's teeth max out at about 3 inches (7.6 cm).

ACTUAL SIZE!
5 INCHES
(12.7 CM)

CRUCIFIX FISH

Saltwater catfish are also known as "crucifix fish" thanks to the shape of a cross that appears on the underside of their skulls. These bones are frequently collected and used as decoration by people of the Christian faith in parts of South and Central America, as well as Gulf Coast states like Mississippi.

SHIPWORM FOSSIL

Shipworms are a type of clam that bore into wood submerged in saltwater, using it for both food and shelter. They have existed for millions of years, as shown by this fossilized evidence of their snacking. Sometimes called the "termites of the sea," shipworms can fill wooden boats and docks with hundreds of holes, making them unstable and prone to sinking or collapsing.

ALL MADE UP

Mimi Choi traded in her day job as a preschool teacher to pursue a career in illusion makeup, and the eye-twisting results appear straight out of Salvador Dalí's playbook.

Mimi has gained acclaim for her 3D makeup effects, enhanced by her ability to create illusions that look shockingly realistic. At the 2019 Met Gala, she gave Ezra Miller one of her signature "multi-feature" looks, endowing him with seven eyes and as many eyebrows. Her mind-boggling skills and trippy take on fashion have caught the attention of many in the industry. She boasts partnerships with Make Up For Ever and MAC, and if her more than 1.7 million followers on Instagram are any indication, we'll be seeing a lot more of her eye-catching creations.

LOOK CLOSELY!

INDEX

PAGE NUMBERS IN ITALIC REFER TO IMAGES.

ESCAPE THE

Make memories that will last a lifetime at a Ripley's Attraction near you! From mind-boggling museums to heart-pounding experiences and awe-inspiring aquariums, find them all at Ripleys.com.

Connect with the stories of unbelievable people and extraordinary things through hands-on interactives, one-of-a-kind exhibits, fun photo opportunities, and much more! You have to see it to believe it at Ripley's Believe It or Not! Odditoriums!

ORDINARY

Featuring underwater habitats from around the globe, Ripley's Aquariums allow you to get face-to-fin with thousands of fascinating fish and remarkable creatures thriving in our world-class facilities.

ACKNOWLEDGMENTS

Master graphics Luis Fuentes, © Andrey_Kuzmin/Shutterstock.com, © Color Symphony/Shutterstock.com, © Miubewa/Shutterstock.com, © Kirill.Veretennikov/Shutterstock.com, © hero mujahid/Shutterstock.com **10** (t) Courtesy Jingsong, (cl) Ripley Entertainment, Inc., (cr) © NK-55/Shutterstock.com, (bl) Courtesy Rachel Knauss, (br) Mimi Choi (@mimles) **11** (tl) Courtesy Werner Härtle and Peter von Felbert www.felbert.de, (r) © Christophe Cappelli/Shutterstock.com, (cl) Courtesy Cedric Laquieze, (c) Courtesy Grace Good. Photos by Hannah Meredith Photography, Verse Concepts, Saiza Photography, and Kurtis Downs., (b) Courtesy Christopher Van Wyk **12–13** (t) The Plexiglass Pontiac, 1940, Wyland Stanley collection at Shorpy.com **12** (b) The Lyda Hill Texas Collection of Photographs in Carol M. Highsmith's America Project, Library of Congress, Prints and Photographs Division. **13** (b) Courtesy Rachel Knauss **14–15** Duke Marine Robotics and Remote Sensing, MarineUAS.net **16** (tr) © Peyker/Shutterstock.com, (cl) © JIANG HONGYAN/Shutterstock.com, (l) "Ivan the Terrible" by Viktor Vasnetsov. Public domain., (b) "Mary Tudor, Queen of England, Second Wife of Philip II" by Anthonis Mor. Public domain. **17** (tl) Alto Vintage Images/Alamy Stock Photo, (tr) BTEU/AUSMUM/Alamy Stock Photo, (bl) Yogi Black/Alamy Stock Photo, (br) markferguson2/Alamy Stock Photo **18** (t) © retirementbonus/Shutterstock.com, (c) © Joyce LCY/Shutterstock.com **19** © oliverfoerschner/Shutterstock.com **20–21** Courtesy Tonje Halvorsen **21** (tr) Roger-Viollet/TopFoto **22** (t) Etienne Littlefair/Nature Picture Library, (b) © NataliaCatalina/Shutterstock.com **23** (bkg) © NK-55/Shutterstock.com, (t) © Henri Koskinen/Shutterstock.com **26** SWNS **27** (t) NASA, (bl) NASA, (br) NASA **30** thrillerfillerspiller/Alamy Stock Photo **31** (bkg) REUTERS/Alessandro Bianchi/Alamy Stock Photo, (tr) REUTERS/Alessandro Bianchi/Alamy Stock Photo **32** (tl) Ingo Arndt/Nature Picture Library/Alamy Stock Photo, (tr) © Beatrice Tan/Shutterstock.com, (bl) © natfu/Shutterstock.com, (br) Kim Taylor/Nature Picture Library **33** (tl) Marine Explorer via Flickr (CC BY-NC-SA 2.0), (tr) Helmut Corneli/Alamy Stock Photo, (b) © lucky vectorstudio/Shutterstock.com **34–35** (t) Courtesy Tori Kubick. Photography by Patrick Jansen and Edrick Krozendijk **34** (bl) J E E/SIPA/Shutterstock.com, (br) J E E/SIPA/Shutterstock.com **35** br Courtesy Samuel Marshall **36** © HelloRF Zcool/Shutterstock.com **37** Courtesy of Dunking Devils **38–39** www.peterszucsy.com **40** Tampa Bay Times/ZUMA Wire/Alamy Live News **41** REUTERS/Gleb Garanich/Alamy Stock Photo **42** (tr) Courtesy of Townsville Enterprise **42** (b) Peter Macdiarmid/Shutterstock **43** SWNS **44** (tl) CNMages/Alamy Stock Photo, (b) Unknown/Alamy Stock Photo **45** (tl) PooMuseum via Wikimedia Commons (CC BY-SA 4.0), (tr) Dan Leeth/Alamy Stock Photo, (cr) © JKI14/Shutterstock.com, (b) Leigh Henningham/Alamy Stock Photo **46** Courtesy Malan Hughes **47** @gusdogtheboston/Caters News **48** (t) Library of Congress, Bain Collection. LC-B2- 2687-1, (c) Library of Congress, Bain Collection. LC-B2- 2473-9, (b) Library of Congress, Bain Collection. LC-B2- 2473-10 **49** (t) EMILY KASK/AFP via Getty Images, (b) Darrellrhodesmiller via Flickr (CC BY-NC 2.0) **50** Photo by Rodrigo Cabadas Trejo **51** Courtesy Nicolas Gentile **54** (t) © dvande/Shutterstock.com **55** Danté Fenolio/Science Source **56–57** Mo. Creates **57** (b) Photo by Dave Killen/The Oregonian **58** (t) Pal Hermansen/Nature Picture Library, (b) North Wind Picture Archives/Alamy Stock Photo **59** Courtesy of the Getty's Open Content Program **60–61** James Schwabel/Alamy Stock Photo **61** (t) LeighMcB via Flickr (CC BY-NC-SA 2.0), (b) Courtesy Michael Foley DMD **62** (t) PR Image Factory/Shutterstock.com, (c) Lapina/Shutterstock.com, (b) © LightField Studios/Shutterstock.com **63** (t) © Estrada Anton/Shutterstock.com, (cl) © Exclusive Pictures/Shutterstock.com, (cr) © Han_eck/Shutterstock.com **64** (t) WAYHOME studio/Shutterstock.com **65** (t) Tsewang Gurmet/Shutterstock.com **66–67** Courtesy Werner Härtle and Peter von Felbert www.felbert.de **68** (t) blickwinkel/Alamy Stock Photo, (b) Chris Hellier/Alamy Stock Photo **69** Sarah Carey/University of Florida **70** Chen Qing/VCG via Getty Images **71** doooo/MOTHER FACTORY **74** (tl, tr) Michelle Nguyen/Cover-Images.com, (b) Frank Rumpenhorst/dpa/Alamy Live News **75** CHRISTOPHE ARCHAMBAULT/AFP via Getty Images **76** (l) © Zoran Karapancev/Shutterstock.com, (r) © Olga Lyubochkina/Shutterstock.com **77** © mundosemfim/Shutterstock.com **78** (t) © Guajillo studio/Shutterstock.com, (b) Courtesy Rachel Knauss **79** (tl, tr) Wolfgang Steiner/Alamy Stock Photo, (b) Guo Chen/Xinhua/Alamy Live News **80–81** Andy Rouse/Nature Picture Library **81** Charlie Summers/Nature Picture Library **82** (t) GIUSEPPE CACACE/AFP via Getty Images, (c) Deep Dive Dubai/Cover Images **82–83** (b) PA Images/Alamy Stock Photo, (t) Deep Dive Dubai/Cover Images **84** (t) agefotostock/Alamy Stock Photo, (c) TOLGA AKMEN/AFP via Getty Images, (b) Guy Corbishley/Alamy Stock Photo **85** Courtesy Manel De Aguas and Marcelina Dvorak **86** (tr) 71-1250, Houghton Library, Harvard University. Public domain., (cl) Nye, C. J. Courtesy of the Alaska Volcano Observatory/Alaska Division of Geological & Geophysical Surveys, (bl) Glicken, Harry. Public domain., (br) © danterd/Shutterstock.com **87** (tl) © Stereo Lights/Shutterstock.com, (cl) Andrew Mason/a_mason via Flickr (CC BY 2.0), (cr) Favisel_Raven/Shutterstock.com, (br) Courtesy Chris Roberts-Antieau and Sarah Taylor, Antieau Gallery **89** Laurel Cunningham-Hill Capsulariums.com **90** Courtesy Rocky Stoutenburgh **91** Airbnb/Cover Images **93** (t) Reserve Bank of Zimbabwe. Public Domain. **94** (t) Nature Picture Library/Alamy Stock Photo, (b) © RudiErnst/Shutterstock.com **95** Courtesy Canis Dosemeci **97** (cr, cl) © Great Prints Philippines/Shutterstock.com, (b) SOPA Images Limited/Alamy Stock Photo, (b) REUTERS/Romeo Ranoco/Alamy Stock Photo **96–97** Ania Blazejewska/Getty Images **98** (t) Stefano Mazzola/Awakening/Getty Images, (b) SWNS **99** (bl) © Anne Richard/Shutterstock.com, (t) © GagliardiPhotography/Shutterstock.com, (br) Jason Ogulnik/Alamy Stock Photo **100** (t) John Robert McPherson via Wikimedia (CC BY-SA 4.0), (b) © Chris Watson/Shutterstock.com **101** Courtesy Inhee Lee **102** (t) © Oleg Kormushin/Shutterstock.com, (c) sporkist via Flickr (CC BY 2.0), (b) © Nagel Photography/Shutterstock.com **103** (tr) © Jam Travels/Shutterstock.com, (tcl) © SMAJC/Shutterstock.com, (bcl) © saiko3p/Shutterstock.com, (c) Danny Ye/Shutterstock.com, (b) Per Olof Forsberg via Flickr (CC BY 2.0) **104** (t) EVGENIY SOFRONEYEV/AFP via Getty Images, (b) MOHAMMED MAHJOUB/AFP via Getty Images **105** (t) Ayaal Fedorov/Just Create/Cover-Images.com, (b) REUTERS/Kim Kyung-Hoon **106–107** (bkg) © saiko3p/Shutterstock.com **106** (t) © MBV1/Shutterstock.com, (b) © Christophe Cappelli/Shutterstock.com **107** (t) © Steve Allen/Shutterstock.com, (b) © Oleg Znamenskiy/Shutterstock.com **108** SWNS **109** Courtesy Gioni Gessele **110** (t) Chen Lee/Minden Pictures, (c) © Jean-Edouard Rozey/Shutterstock.com **110–111** Courtesy Scott Gardner **112** Krill Design/Cover Images **113** (t) Gorham and Company, Missouri History Museum via Wikimedia (Public Domain), (bl) Chronicle/Alamy Stock Photo, (c) U.S. Army photo by Elizabeth Fraser/Arlington National Cemetery (Public Domain) **116–117** RealyEasyStar/Daniele Bellucci/Alamy Stock Photo **118** (t) Henning Bagger/EPA-EFE/Shutterstock, (b) © Travelvolo/Shutterstock.com **119** (t) sutsaiy/Shutterstock.com, (c) © Decha Thapanya/Shutterstock.com **120** (tl) © Faviel_Raven/Shutterstock.com, (bl) © Tara Lynn and Co/Shutterstock.com **121** (c) © Wang LiQiang/Shutterstock.com, (b) Granitethighs via Wikimedia Commons (CC BY-SA 3.0) **121** BIOSPHOTO/Alamy Stock Photo, (b) REUTERS/Alamy Stock Photo **122** (t) Frags of Life via Flickr (CC BY-NC-SA 2.0), (b) Peter Atkinson/Alamy Stock Photo **123** CHRISTIAN BRUNA/EPA-EFE/Shutterstock **124** Courtesy Midhun RR **125** (tr) PA Images/Alamy Stock Photo, (b) Aidan Meller/Cover-Images.com **126** (t) SWNS, (b) © Anja Denker/Solent News & Photo Agency **127** Rebecca Krebs, North Star Poultry **128** (c) © EWY Media/Shutterstock.com, (t) Zavijava2 via Wikimedia (CC BY-SA 3.0) **129** (t) © StrippedPixel.com, (bkg, br) © Wang Sing/Shutterstock.com **130–131** Courtesy Ali Spagnola **132** Courtesy Jingsong **133** Courtesy Dominik Arend **136** (t) PA Images/Alamy Stock Photo, (b) Hawkes Lab/UCSB/Cover-Images.com **137** Courtesy Indy Voet **138–139** Courtesy Mark Verge **140** (t) National Archives and Records Administration, 533758. Public domain., (b) Library of Congress, Detroit Publishing Company photograph collection, LC-D4-17130. Public domain. **141** Hap/Quirky China News/Shutterstock **142** (b) Chris Melzer/dpa picture alliance/Alamy Stock Photo **143** (c) Gehad Hamdy/dpa picture alliance/Alamy Stock Photo, (b) Jonathan Rashad/Getty Images **144–145** (t) Courtesy of Judy Fridono, SurfDogRicochet.com, social media @surfdogricochet. Photography by Rob Ochoa and Heather Moana. **145** (b) SWNS **146** (cl) Nutu/Alamy Stock Photo, (tr, cr) Abaca Press/Alamy Stock Photo **146** (b) Nayeryouakim via Wikimedia Commons (CC BY-SA 4.0) **147** (tl) © DnDavis/Shutterstock.com, (tr) © CloudOnePhoto/Shutterstock.com, (cl) Jack Versloot via Flickr (CC BY 2.0), (cr) © Dylan.King/Shutterstock.com, (b) © alisafarov/Shutterstock.com **148–149** VICKIE FLORES/EPA-EFE/Shutterstock **149** (t) Claudia Greco/AGF/Shutterstock, (b) Chris Jackson/Getty Images **150** (t) Collection of National Media Museum. Public domain., (b) © FabricioUZ/Shutterstock.com **151** (t) PA Images/Alamy Stock Photo, (b) amer ghazzal/Alamy Stock Photo **152** Janine Pendleton (Obsidian Urbex Photography) **153** (t) Wil Elrick & Kelly Kazek KellyKazek.com, (bl) Sam Howzit via Flickr (CC BY 2.0), (cr, br) James Schwabel/Alamy Stock Photo **154** Collection of the Bata Shoe Museum. Copyright © 2022 Bata Shoe Museum, Toronto, Canada **155** (bkg) The Natural History Museum/Alamy Stock Photo, (cr) Steve White of The Great Canadian Flea Circus and Flea and Insect Museum **158–159** Courtesy Leanne "Elrod" Rodriguez **160** (t) Avalon.red/Alamy Stock Photo, (cr, br) SWNS **161** (t) FREDERIC BROWN/AFP via Getty Images, (br) Horniman Museum and Gardens via Flickr (CC BY-NC 2.0) **162** (bkg) © Taromon/Shutterstock.com, (tr) irisphotos via Flickr (CC BY-ND 2.0) **163** (tl) Inge Johnsson/Alamy Stock Photo, (c) Jinrui Qu via Flickr (CC BY-SA 2.0), (tr) Courtesy Francis McEachern **164** (t) © Roy Palmer/Shutterstock.com, (tr) © Jota_Visual/Shutterstock.com, (b) Rob Lavinsky, iRocks.com (CC-BY-SA-3.0) **165** (tr) Hendrik Schmidt/dpa-Zentralbild/ZB/dpa/Alamy Live News, (cl) © Dafinchi/Shutterstock.com, (cr) © Albert Russ/Shutterstock.com, (b) Charles D. Winters/Science Source **166** (t) Hector Vivas/Getty Images, (b) Courtesy Kathy Tate Davis **167** Koji Ueda/AP/Shutterstock **168** (l) Courtesy of Anna Zora, Justin Gerlach, Fregate Island **168–169** Courtesy Melissa Arleth and Joseph Frazz Photography **170–171** Photo by MikeHebergerPhoto.com, courtesy Tony DeMatteo www.HalloweenOnAmbush.com **172** Martin Child/Getty Images **173** Anthony Baker/Alamy Stock Photo **174–175** @trademeproject **178–179** Courtesy Stefanie Millinger, photos by Julian Artner/@julian_artner **179** PinPep/Shutterstock **180–181** Dgtmedia – Simone via Wikimedia (CC BY 3.0) **180** (t) © MikeDotta/Shutterstock.com, (bl, br) SWNS **181** Keystone-France/Gamma-Keystone via Getty Images **182** (tl) Photo by Wednesday Aja, courtesy of Venardos Circus, (tr) Photo by Eric Forrest, courtesy of Venardos Circus, (bl, br) Photo by Jasmine Ellsworth, courtesy of Venardos Circus **183** (t) Photo by Jasmine Ellsworth, courtesy of Venardos Circus **183** (tr) Photo by Eric Forrest, courtesy of Venardos Circus **184** (tl) David Fleetham/Alamy Stock Photo **184–185** Nature Picture Library/Alamy Stock Photo **185** (tr) © Agnieszka Bacal/Shutterstock.com **186** Caviar/Cover Images **187** SWNS **188** Klein Vision/Cover-Images.com **189** (t) Vilnius Tech Linkmenu Fabrikas/Cover Images, (b) © Alberto Tiano/Shutterstock.com **190** (tr, bl) © a katz/Shutterstock.com, (br) REUTERS/Evelyn Hockstein/Alamy Stock Photo **191** (tl) © a katz/Shutterstock.com, (tr) © MAHATHIR MOHD YASIN/Shutterstock.com, (b) © Hortimages/Shutterstock.com, (br) Anthony Behar/Sipa USA/Alamy Stock Photo **192** Courtesy Electronicos Fantasticos and Mao Yamamoto **193** (t) kevin Hodgson/Alamy Stock Photo, (b) Paul Goldstein/Cover-Images.com **194–195** Royal Geographical Society/Alamy Stock Photo **195** (t) © Robbie Fatt/Shutterstock.com **198** © Karlheinz Reichert/Shutterstock.com **199** (t) © Somogyi Laszlo/Shutterstock.com, (c) © Nigel Housden/Shutterstock.com, (bl) © Rudmer Zwerver/Shutterstock.com, (br) www.norfolkislandtime.com.au **200** JOHAN ORDONEZ/AFP via Getty Images **201** Clara Gamito/Alamy Stock Photo **202** (tr) Chen Yuyu/VCG via Getty Images, (b) Xing Yun/Costfoto/Barcroft Media via Getty Images **203** (t) Phil Walter/Getty Images, (b) Dave Rowland/Getty Images for the New Zealand Olympic Committee **204–205** Courtesy of the Nantucket Historical Association **206** New England Wildlife Centers **207** (t) AG News/Alamy Stock Photo, (bl) © Dirk Ercken/Shutterstock.com **208** (tr) John Locher/AP/Shutterstock, (cl) © WAYHOME studio/Shutterstock.com, (br) James Atoa/UPI/Alamy Stock Photo **209** (tl) LARRY W SMITH/EPA-EFE/Shutterstock, (tr) Shizuo Kambayashi/AP/Shutterstock, (blc) © Kovalchuk Oleksandr/Shutterstock.com, (b) © paffy/Shutterstock.com, (br) Ethan Miller/Getty Images **210** SWNS **211** (t) © ivan canavera/Shutterstock.com, (bkg) Kristel Richard/Nature Picture Library **214** (t) Stephen Chung/Alamy Stock Photo, (bl, br) SWNS **215** (t) Grant Walker/Cover Images, (b) AGAMI Photo Agency/Alamy Stock Photo **216–217** Courtesy Grace Good. Photos by Hannah Meredith Photography, Verse Concepts, Saiza Photography, and Kurtis Downs. **218** REUTERS/Soe Zeya Tun/Alamy Stock Photo **219** (t) Konstantin Labunskiy/Alamy Stock Photo, (b) REUTERS/Maxim Shemetov/Alamy Stock Photo **220** (t) patrickkavanagh via Flickr (CC BY 2.0), (c) © Joa Souza/Shutterstock.com, (b) Paulo de Oliveira/Minden Pictures **221** (t) © Thorsten Spoerlein/Shutterstock.com, (cl) © RealityImages/Shutterstock.com, (bl) © Aniek_S/Shutterstock.com, (cr) © Juergen Freund/Nature Picture Library **222–223** (t) REUTERS/Peter Cziborra/Alamy Stock Photo **222** (b) Herve BRUHAT/Gamma-Rapho via Getty Images **223** (t) REUTERS/Ivan Alvarado/Alamy Stock Photo, (b) STR/JIJI PRESS/AFP via Getty Image **224** © 2021, California State Parks. All rights reserved. **225** (t) © Greg Amptman/Shutterstock.com, (bl) STEFAN SAUER/dpa/Alamy Stock Photo, (br) © IrinaK/Shutterstock.com **226** (t) PA Images/Alamy Stock Photo, (bl) Ian Pilbeam/Alamy Stock Photo **227** SWNS **228–229** House – Kelly Little-Kuehnert, Installation @littlekuehnert / Dolls – Lillian Bass / Addams Car – Vanessa Busti / Commissioned by Linda LaPage **230** Alexis Rosenfeld/Getty Images **231** (t) Sakchai Lalit/AP/Shutterstock, (b) Alexis Rosenfeld/Getty Images **232** (t) Natural History Collection/Alamy Stock Photo, (c) © Brian L. Lambert/Shutterstock.com **233** (t) Courtesy Christopher Van Wyk, (c) © Hamik/Shutterstock.com, (cr) © Ewa Studio/Shutterstock.com, (b) Farlap/Alamy Stock Photo **234** (tr) Bernhard Sobotta/Cercle the World/Cover-images.com **234** (cl, b) Brenda Thompson/SpecialFinds.com/Cover Images **235** (t) © leshiy985/Shutterstock.com, (b) © C. Na Songkhla/Shutterstock.com **236–237** Courtesy Cedric Laquieze **237** (tl) © Margus Vilbas Photography/Shutterstock.com, (cl) © BenjieStudio/Shutterstock.com, (bl) © Vladimirkarp/Shutterstock.com **238–239** © Esin Deniz/Shutterstock.com **238** (b) © emasali stock/Shutterstock.com **239** (t) PADMANABHA RAO/AFP via Getty Images **240** Richard Lautens/Toronto Star via Getty Images **241** Kearney & Associates Realty **243** (t) Matthew R McClure/Shutterstock.com, (cb) Frank Hecker/Alamy Stock Photo **244–245** Mimi Choi (@mimles) **245** © leisuretime70/Shutterstock.com

Key: t = top, b = bottom, c = center, l = left, r = right, bkg = background

All other photos are from Ripley Entertainment, Inc. Every attempt has been made to acknowledge correctly and contact copyright holders and we apologize in advance for any unintentional errors or omissions, which will be corrected in future editions.

CONNECT WITH Ripley's ONLINE OR IN PERSON

28
EXTRAORDINARY LOCATIONS

There are 28 incredible Ripley's Believe It or Not! Odditoriums all around the world, where you can experience our spectacular collection!

Amsterdam THE NETHERLANDS	**Copenhagen** DENMARK	**Hollywood** CALIFORNIA	**Orlando** FLORIDA	**Surfers Paradise** AUSTRALIA
Atlantic City NEW JERSEY	**Dubai** UNITED ARAB EMIRATES	**Mexico City** MEXICO	**Panama City Beach** FLORIDA	**Veracruz** MEXICO
Blackpool ENGLAND	**Gatlinburg** TENNESSEE	**Myrtle Beach** SOUTH CAROLINA	**Pattaya** THAILAND	**Williamsburg** VIRGINIA
Branson MISSOURI	**Genting Highlands** MALAYSIA	**Newport** OREGON	**San Antonio** TEXAS	**Wisconsin Dells** WISCONSIN
Cancún MEXICO	**Grand Prairie** TEXAS	**Niagara Falls** ONTARIO, CANADA	**San Francisco** CALIFORNIA	
Cavendish P.E.I., CANADA	**Guadalajara** MEXICO	**Ocean City** MARYLAND	**St. Augustine** FLORIDA	

Stop by our website for new stories, contests, and more! **www.ripleys.com**
Don't forget to connect with us on social media for a daily dose of the weird and the wonderful.

 /RipleysBelieveItorNot @Ripleys youtube.com/Ripleys

 @RipleysBelieveItorNot  @ripleysbelieveitornot